Corporate Strategy in the Age of Responsibility

To all those in business, consultancy and academia who seek a new direction for corporate strategy

Corporate Strategy in the Age of Responsibility

PETER MCMANNERS

Henley Business School, University of Reading, UK

Routledge
Taylor & Francis Group

LONDON AND NEW YORK

First published 2014 by Gower Publishing

2 Park Square, Milton Park, Abingdon, Oxfordshire OX14 4RN
52 Vanderbilt Avenue, New York, NY 10017

Routledge is an imprint of the Taylor & Francis Group, an informa business

First issued in paperback 2020

Gower Applied Business Research
Our programme provides leaders, practitioners, scholars and researchers with thought provoking, cutting edge books that combine conceptual insights, interdisciplinary rigour and practical relevance in key areas of business and management.

British Library Cataloguing in Publication Data
A catalogue record for this book is available from the British Library.

Library of Congress Cataloging-in-Publication Data
McManners, Peter J.
  Corporate strategy in the age of responsibility / by Peter McManners.
    pages cm
  Includes bibliographical references and index.
  ISBN 978-1-4724-2360-3 (hardback)
  1. International business enterprises--Management. 2. Strategic
  planning. 3. Sustainable development--International cooperation. I. Title.
  HD62.4.M3965 2014
  658.4'012--dc23

                                                                                    2014005407

ISBN 978-1-4724-2360-3 (hbk)
ISBN 978-0-367-60617-6 (pbk)

CONTENTS

LIST OF FIGURES

LIST OF TABLES

LIST OF BOXES

LIST OF ABBREVIATIONS

CEO	Chief Executive Officer
COP	Conference of the Parties
CSR	Corporate Social Responsibility
DNA	Deoxyribonucleic acid
ESCO	Energy Service Company
EU	European Union
EWEA	European Wind Energy Association
GDP	Gross Domestic Product
GSM	Global System for Mobile Communications
IPCC	Intergovernmental Panel on Climate Change
IT	Information Technology
JV	Joint Venture
MBA	Master of Business Administration
MBO	Management Buy-out
MNC	Multinational Corporation
NGO	Non-governmental organisation
OFT	Office of Fair Trading

OPEC   Organization of the Petroleum Exporting Countries

ORR   Office of Rail Regulation

PESTEL   Political, Economic, Social, Technology, Environment and Legal

POS   Prime Opportunity Space

PPI   Payment Protection Insurance

RBS   Royal Bank of Scotland

ROI   Return on Investment

SOS   Shared Operating Space

UCS   Unique Competing Space

UK   United Kingdom

UNFCCC   United Nations Framework Convention on Climate Change

VC   Venture Capitalist

WTO   World Trade Organization

FOREWORD

The corporation is the engine of capitalism mobilising resources to deliver products and services that support society and, as such, their behaviour and ways of doing business are vital to the success of capitalist economies. Of great concern is the evidence that the corporate agenda and the needs of society have taken divergent paths. One much discussed issue is that executives are being encouraged or even forced to focus on short-term profit, by stakeholders demanding an immediate return, and fuelled by remuneration packages based primarily on delivering uplift in share price. These pressures can, of course, engender sub-optimal corporate behaviour, particularly in regard to the corporation's wider role within society.

Looking beyond narrow corporate boundaries, governments face huge emerging challenges such as how to make the transition to a low-carbon economy. The solution to these may require changes to the basis of capitalism or, more likely, may require a quite different system of government-based rewards and threats to corporations than is currently in place. This combination of a myopic focus on the bottom line and failure to engage with the huge emerging challenges faced by government is the gap between the corporation and the needs of society. This book is about bringing the corporation back to its rightful place at the heart of society tackling the issues which matter, delivering solutions – and generating a profit.

As the Dean of Henley Business School, I am delighted to write the foreword to a book which echoes the ethos on which we were founded. Henley was established in 1945 to satisfy the need for capable, professional managers to rebuild the economy following World War Two. Responsibility was a non-negotiable assumption that underpinned all that was taught. This management approach continues today with 'honest profit' remaining as one of our core values. Responsibility is not an optional extension to the corporate financial model but lies at the heart of long-term commercial success. When corporations lose track of this, it is the beginning of their demise.

Peter McManners provides not only a blueprint for formulating strategy, but also a framework which supports engagement with the emerging issues which will shape the economy in the decades ahead. He challenges deep-rooted assumptions about business-as-usual, in order to reform, rebuild and reinforce the corporation. Extrapolation of current trends leads to anodyne strategy; the strategic approach presented here has the potential to steer the corporation into a secure place at the core of fulfilling society's current and future needs.

This book is published at a time when the motives of business are being questioned; by governments who have had to deal with the consequences of corporate failings; by NGOs critical of corporate behaviour; and customers who fear they are being exploited. Rebuilding trust in the corporation requires a different approach to strategy. This is not about blunting commercial discipline but is all about honest profit from mobilising corporate capabilities to serve society with appropriate solutions. The ideas and methodology presented are designed to suit the emerging challenges of the twenty-first century. This is the right book, at the right time it deserves to be read widely within business, consultancy and business schools to stimulate discussion about the need for changes to the rules of the corporate game.

John Board
Dean
Henley Business School
Reading University
United Kingdom

PREFACE

The strategic process presented in this book is a practitioner's guide to exploiting the new realities of the twenty-first century. Major change is coming as the global economy hits resource limits at a point not too far into the future. This is likely to coincide with the consequences of climate change reaching a level of severity to force governments to take action. The strategy formulation presented in this book is for the new era of altered priorities. It is not a strategy for sustainability or a manifesto for green business, although these issues feature prominently, but core business strategy as it should be carried out to fit with the challenges and opportunities of this age. The coming revolution will be every bit as dramatic as the Industrial Revolution of the nineteenth century or the Information Revolution of the twentieth century. The Sustainable Revolution[1] will require different thinking to align corporate strategy with these emerging challenges.

The methods of strategic analysis can be used across all business sectors for all sizes of firm by management, management consultants and for teaching business strategy to MBA level. The methodology is compatible with mainstream conventional strategic thinking expanded to bring the concepts of sustainability inside the analytic frame. Practitioners can choose how far and how fast they shift from the old school of competitive strategy focussed on bottom-line performance to embrace the paradigm presented here of cementing the corporation at the heart of society working alongside government. This book is not so much a new approach as taking management back to its roots as a vital and responsible part of Western civilisation, playing a full role in society and respected for its ability to make people's lives better.

In Part I, the reader is challenged to consider leaving the comfort zone of assuming the continuation of the macroeconomic policies of recent decades. In Parts II and

---

1   The coming revolution will acquire an agreed name in history books written in the future. The economist Nicholas Stern has described it as the 'Global Low-carbon Industrial Revolution' (Stern 2010) but that does not reflect the breadth and scale of the coming revolution. Throughout this book the term 'Sustainable Revolution' is used, taken from the book *Adapt and Thrive: The Sustainable Revolution* (McManners 2008).

III, the core strategic process is described and explained with implementation covered in Part IV. The impatient reader, under personal or external pressure to move fast, could skip over Part I and start with Part II. However this could miss important insights. Strategy that is successful over the long-term requires careful analysis, deep thought and deliberate reflection. Part I sets the context for such an analysis by examining how the world is changing. You may not agree with all the predictions but by accepting the context of change, it opens the door to crafting strategy that bucks the status quo and places the business at the forefront of some highly lucrative opportunities. If you choose to ignore the context presented in Part I you will not be alone; most of the corporate world is placing their bets on the continuation of the status quo, or something very much like the status quo. Setting strategy which conflicts with conventional wisdom carries risk, and may not suit every business and will certainly meet resistance in the boardroom. This book encourages practitioners to include novel strategic options for consideration even if the final selection by the Board plumps for something less ambitious and less contentious.

Strategy should not be about codifying what everybody expects but should challenge management to consider alternative directions. Following the process presented in this book will, at the very least, feed some novel ideas into the boardroom but could launch corporate strategy to the forefront of the next big thing: The Sustainable Revolution.

Peter McManners

INTRODUCTION

Crafting winning corporate strategy has never been easy but it is about to get a whole lot more complicated. The challenge of retaining economic stability as resource limits are reached, and the consequences of climate change hit home, will shake the foundations of the corporate world. The disruption will generate huge opportunities which can be exploited if business leaders have the foresight and courage to take off the blinkers of orthodox corporate strategy and are willing to adopt a different mind-set. The facts of climate change are broadly accepted and although at global level there is no workable plan of action, the fact that there must be change to the fossil-fuel economy is clear. The defenders of the status quo are now few and are becoming marginalized. Europe may have been the incubator for sustainability policy but the tide may turn away from Europe, where there has been early progress, to the United States as the Republican Party shifts its position removing a key block to action. In China, the leadership has made clear its intention to clean up its act and stake a claim to the new low-carbon economy. The scene is set for radical change across all markets as the policy framework is reconfigured, partly through deliberate policy but mainly through the unstoppable force of circumstances beyond government and corporate control.

Many of the world's largest corporations were founded in the late nineteenth century at the time of Industrial Revolution. Since 1990, the Information Revolution has reconfigured the corporate space forcing fundamental corporate re-engineering and spawning a new wave of corporations including recent arrivals on the corporate scene, Google and Facebook. The Sustainable Revolution will be equally seismic; corporations must respond or risk getting frozen out of the new economy. There is a bright and prosperous future for the corporations that lead the transition but many masters of twentieth century capitalism will be toppled as the new reality dawns.

Corporate strategy provides direction and coordination to allow all parts of the corporation to work towards shared aims and objectives. A good strategy succeeds in mobilizing the corporation's resources in response to the challenges and opportunities in the macro business environment within a framework of sound commercial logic. A poor strategy can leave a corporation floundering with each business unit struggling to make a profit as best it can without a core purpose to galvanize the business. Other strategies will fail because, although based on sound analysis of the current industry, they are not suited to the challenges of the future. Contemporary strategy requires deep analysis of the commercial reality of doing business in a complex world facing an uncertain future.

Corporate responsibility is fundamental to long-term success, but in some cases this has been side-lined or forgotten as a narrow focus on delivering shareholder value has come to dominate strategic thinking. There have always been businesses operating on the edge of legality but over the last two decades it has become accepted, almost expected, in some industries, notably parts of banking and financial services, to push the business to the very edge of what is allowed by law in a drive to maximize returns to shareholders. As corporations take deliberate action to find loopholes in legislation, and have few qualms about being disingenuous in their dealings with customers to make sales, the trust of society is evaporating. Many corporations are run in a responsible manner but the extreme bad behaviour of some businesses grabs the headlines and make doing business harder than it needs to be. The endemic problem for the corporate world is a headlong rush to deliver bottom-line profits which has undermined the corporation as a trusted agent within society and challenges the government to tighten the rules. Reversing this trend and rebuilding trust will take time and requires that business demonstrates that it can be trusted once again. Parts of the business community have been the architects of this loss of trust and now the wider corporate community have to pick up the pieces and design a new way forward where responsible behaviour is the normal expected default position.

At this juncture in history, the world faces the multiple challenges of maintaining economic well-being and social cohesion whilst living within planetary limits. The nexus of resource limits, climate change and the threat of economic instability is deeply intractable but also a huge opportunity for those corporations that can deliver the solutions. Becoming indispensable to society is a solid platform from which to generate profits and persuade governments to back off. It is also clear that doing business is easier if society is offered products and services that fit with customers' real needs, and more enduring than chasing the next consumer fad. Responsible corporate strategy may seem like an oxymoron as the world is gripped by consumer capitalism but responsible strategy is the way of the future and the only sure way to underpin long-term corporate success.

In the 1990s, the idea took hold that deregulation would boost the economy through giving business the freedom to operate without hindrance. The core notion that business freed from regulation can be more effective is sound, but the concept has been hijacked over the last two decades by an influential minority of business leaders acting in their own self-interest. For example, Fred Goodwin, CEO of the Royal Bank of Scotland Group (RBS) between 2001 and 2009 took blinkered greed to a new level presiding over the largest annual loss in UK corporate history. In the United States, Richard 'Dick' Fuld, CEO of Lehman Brothers (1994–2008) used his belligerent and uncompromising focus on making profits by any means to sink what had become the fourth-largest investment bank in the US, declaring bankruptcy in 2008. These people may have been exceptionally selfish and incompetent but they were not acting alone. They were the public faces of a cancer growing within corporate culture with the collusion of investors. These individuals may have left the corporate scene but not enough has been done to remove the malignancy.

A response to the perceived problem of greedy executives is the notion that corporations should be operated principally to deliver shareholder value. Shareholder value has become a staple part of teaching in business schools and widely adopted by corporations and investors but has in reality made the problem worse, not better. This measure can be useful, but at the strategic level it can encourage myopic short-termism and distract corporate decision makers away from long-term sustainable solutions. The combination of deregulation with the introduction of the theory of shareholder value has been a corrosive mix causing damage to corporate standards and long-term corporate performance which will take time to correct.

Governments are seeking ways to regain control but are struggling to find solutions as regulations will always be a step behind the corporations which seek to circumvent the rules. They are finding that their power to encourage more responsible behaviour from the corporate community is limited. For example in 2013 the UK government made little headway in a dispute with the big energy companies who were profiting from an imperfect market to maximize the return to their shareholders. The stand-off between government needing to set effective policy and the energy corporations operating to a myopic profit motive was not conducive to brokering a solution. More responsible corporate behaviour may be desired by government; investors and customers can have influence, but the lead has to come from within industry. Governments cannot legislate effectively for responsibility but they can respond, where industry takes the lead, by removing regulations. Governments also own the tough task of planning and implementing a sustainable low-carbon future. This seems impossibly difficult within the restraints of political acceptability and the legislative power at their disposal. Governments need help to keep the lights on through a period of massive change but their most capable agent, business, is sat on the side-lines. The world needs the capability and drive of the business community to engage with the challenges and help to find solutions. Can governments craft a framework that allows business to take on this role? The answer is 'yes' and 'no'. Yes, governments can legislate and set policy but no, it will not be enough. Business that continues to chase its own tail in a search for quick profits operating within the straightjacket of regulation is clearly a dysfunctional arrangement.

The solution to the challenges of our time hinges around being able to live within the finite limits of the planet and the acceptance of the constraints on resource availability that this requires. Greed has delivered economic growth whilst there were ample resources from an open world market. The future is about securing resource flows, implementing circular economies and eliminating fossil fuel. 'Greed is good'[1] could only ever work over a short time horizon and is now shown to be flawed; perhaps the mantra should become 'Green is good' for the new macroeconomic model. However it is right to be sceptical of a green agenda when 'green' has become synonymous with naïve people with a utopian view of the future. The world needs the hard real edge of business to take 'soft green' and transform it into 'real green'.

'Real green' is about living sustainably on a finite planet with policy that reaches across the political divide. A secure social context is desirable of course, and necessary to provide a base from which to address environmental concerns, but issues of fairness and equity should not be confused with the urgent core challenge of finding pragmatic solutions in an imperfect world to the imperative of living within resource and environmental limits.

The solution consists of limited and carefully targeted government regulation giving business the context and freedom to find the most effective solutions. For this to work, business has to become embedded in society and work alongside government. This requires a new approach to corporate strategy that includes a deep re-evaluation of the role of the corporation and how it serves its primary stakeholders. This book presents a methodology that codifies this new approach.

Part I, focusses on the changes in the macro-economy and how this will shape the business landscape. This part may seem alien to readers versed in conventional strategic thinking and, if so, it is possible to move quickly into Part II and return to Part I when there is time to reflect and think deeply about the future. It is argued that the evolving situation presented in Part I will become a significant strategic driver as the economy falters and resource limits are reached, forcing leaders across society to adapt and embrace new thinking as society and the economy are reconfigured to altered circumstances. But the tipping point could still be some years off; so many strategists will be more comfortable working inside the envelope of what they know and expect without taking the risk of assuming that fundamental change is likely. However, for strategists who want to be ahead of the game, Part I provides the foundation for the development of new and novel strategies. Chapter 1 explains the extent to which society depends on business with the scale of the opportunities outlined in Chapter 2. Chapters 3 and 4 cover the changing economic parameters as globalization falters and is replaced by a

---

1   The expression 'Greed is good' was used by the ruthless and greedy corporate raider played by Michael Douglas in the film *Wall Street* (Pressman & Stone 1987).

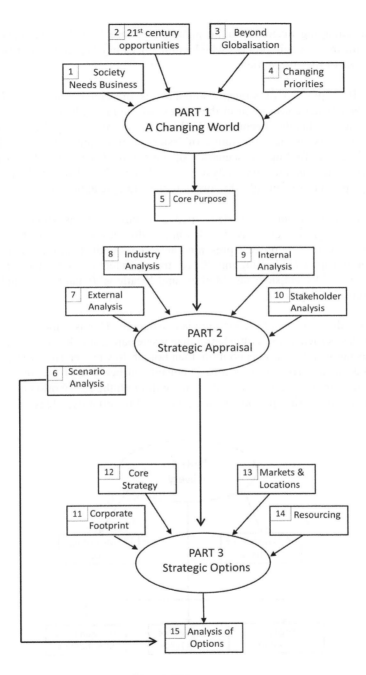

Figure I.1   Book Structure Parts I–III

different emerging macroeconomic paradigm. These first four chapters set the context for the strategic process which commences in Chapter 5 with reassessing the purpose of the corporation.

In Part II, a process of strategic appraisal is presented which examines the capabilities of the corporation in the context of the macro business environment to cultivate insights that become the building blocks of strategy. Chapter 6 opens out the analysis to the wide range of issues surrounding the corporation and encapsulates the findings in scenarios of the future. Chapters 7–10 go through an external analysis, industry analysis, internal analysis and stakeholder analysis, building up a series of insights to complete the strategic appraisal.

In Part III, strategic options are developed using key questions which have served business strategists over many decades but finding a coherent set of answers is increasingly hard. The process presented here starts with 'Defining the corporate footprint' (Chapter 11) leading into 'Core strategy selection' (Chapter 12). Further detail is added by considering 'Markets and locations' (Chapter 13) and finally 'Resourcing' (Chapter 14).

In Part IV, the delivery of the strategy is considered. This is important because a strategy that is filed away is little better than waste paper, and discussion of strategy that does not lead to action is no more than hot air. In Chapter 16, the special case of strategy as a portfolio of options is considered because of the high potential this has to help the executive board navigate through the real-world challenges of implementation during periods of disruption and uncertainty. Measuring success

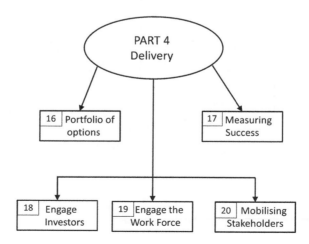

Figure I.2   Structure Part IV

is the theme taken up in Chapter 17 leading to the important issues of engaging investors, the workforce and other stakeholders (Chapters 18–20).

Formulating sound corporate strategy has never been easy, and it has become hugely more challenging with the breadth of issues to consider. The new strategic direction for many corporations is not obvious and may require a step change, but there are massive opportunities for business leaders who can navigate the new landscape successfully. The result can be sustainable and profitable corporations deeply rooted in society and locked into a prosperous future.

PART I

A CHANGING WORLD

*'Management will remain a basic and dominant institution perhaps as long
as Western civilization itself survives'*

Peter Drucker 1955

The corporation does not stand alone but operates within the wider economy exposed to the demands and expectations of society. As the world changes, business must adapt; and business adapts by adopting a new strategic direction. Understanding the changing world in sufficient (but not overwhelming) detail is a fundamental foundation of the strategy formulation process.

The twentieth century saw the emergence of 'management' as a distinct academic discipline and leading institution in industrial and civic society. The influence that management has had – and continues to have – over the direction of society is considerable. The influential management guru Peter Drucker wrote the words above at the time when the first business schools were established with optimism that management would remain a positive force at the heart of Western civilization (Drucker 2007). His view echoes the words of Jonathan Swift three hundred years ago, 'whoever could make two ears of corn, or two blades of grass, to grow upon a spot of ground where only one grew before, [does]... more essential service to his country, than the whole race of politicians put together.' (Swift 1726:223)

In the twenty-first century, corporations have to live up to the aspiration of management as a basic and dominant institution in Western civilization. The world today is subject to huge conflicting pressures as the economy falters and resource limits are reached. This comes at a time when highly populous countries such as India and China aspire to much higher standards of living starting from a very low base. The pressure on resource will be intense. Society is facing an impending crisis but most people have not yet woken up to the enormity of the challenge. Leaders in business and organizations across society need to adapt and embrace new strategic thinking as society and the economy are reconfigured to altered circumstances. The world is at the beginning of a period of massive change and corporate strategy has to move in-step or be left behind. The companies that embrace the emerging new reality have a wealth of opportunities to exploit. Before embarking on a strategic analysis, it is worth climbing up to a high point and looking out across society and the economy to get a feel for the lie of the land and reconsider the core purpose of the corporation.

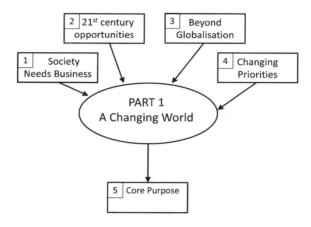

Figure PI.1   Structure Part I

CHAPTER 1

SOCIETY NEEDS BUSINESS

The role of business is as an integral part of society and the economy.

With hindsight, we will look back at the current era and wonder how we can have been so blind to the real world around us; so locked in denial of the need for a new direction; and so completely unable to make the changes required. Each person lives their life within the limits of the possibilities open to them constrained by the bigger picture of society and the economy. Business is similarly constrained, but of all the actors in society, business is the most capable of throwing off the shackles and driving forward the process of change. Society needs business now, more than ever, to take a leading role. If business can show it can be trusted, society will give business permission to operate in new and dramatically different ways. No one should ask, or expect, corporations to become charitable organizations, replacing the profit motive with altruistic intentions, but corporate leaders need the inspiration and freedom to find a new direction for the twenty-first-century corporation. The driver for corporations always has been, and should continue to be, commercial success. Chief executives and senior executives need to take off their blinkers and open their eyes to the emerging new reality. There is a world of commercial opportunities ready to be exploited if business can adapt strategy to address the challenges of our time.

THE ROLE OF BUSINESS

The role of business would seem to be obvious until attempts are made to define it. Does business deliver products and services? Does business provide employment? Does business provide a return to shareholders? Can business do all of this and more? Wherever there is an activity that can be carried out profitably, business will be there, but a generic description of the role of business is elusive.

One starting point is to define what business is not; business is not the government and business is not a charity. Business is not responsible for deciding what is right for society and does not have to step in to cure the ills of society. Perhaps business is simply a mechanism to make money. Is the definition of a successful business a collection of activities which pays out more than you put in? On this basis, a Ponzi[1] scheme would be a good business up to the point where it implodes. Clearly this is not right; business has to have a future that goes beyond an immediate profit. What of a business that delivers a financial profit but causes damage to society or the environment? This would fit the definition of a money-making machine but common sense tells us that this is wrong; such a business is unlikely to last and is at risk of being shut down.

A definition that gets close to capturing the essence of business is:

> *Business is a collection of activities that together fills a role in the economy that is needed by society, which operates within the safe bounds of the environment, and delivers a return to its shareholders.*

This definition appears closer to reality than the idea of business as a money-making machine but this is starting to encroach on areas which are the responsibility of government and overlap with the interest of charitable organizations. We have already decided that business is not governmental or charitable so what is going on?

Business is the universal agent within the capitalist economy. Proponents of free-market capitalism argue that government should get out of the way. Business will arise wherever there is a need; expand and grow where there is demand; and contract and die when the service is no longer needed or is replaced by something better. This philosophy requires government to step back and give business the freedom to operate with the minimum of interference and minimum regulation. Where business uses its freedom responsibly, society is content to renew its licence to operate. However, where business falls into the trap of regarding its activities as little more than making money, the government is forced to step in to legislate. The battle between money-making machines on one side and legislators on the other leads to ever more red tape as the legislator is always one step behind the machine operators. Money-machine-operator mentality kept in line by regulators closing loopholes is no way to manage the primary agents of capitalism.

The role of business is as an integral part of society and the economy. Its freedom to operate correlates directly with the responsibility of its performance. A free

---

1   A Ponzi scheme is a fraudulent investment operation named after Charles Ponzi, who became notorious for using the technique in 1920 (Peck 2011). Such schemes pay high returns to investors from existing capital or new capital paid by new investors, rather than from profits. The perpetuation of the high returns requires an ever-increasing flow of money from new investors to sustain the scheme until there are no more new investors and the scheme collapses.

license to operate is better for business and more responsive to the needs of society but is only granted where business can demonstrate responsible behaviour.

BUSINESS AND SOCIETY

The main actors in society are government, business and a collection of not-for-profit organizations which can be referred to as the 'third sector'. These have different abilities and priorities. The most capable is business, being very good at spotting the opportunities, assessing the risk and mobilizing capital to get things done. Government is the most powerful, operating under the overarching objective of making life better for its people. The third sector fills gaps, operating in a variety of ways depending on the organization's charitable objectives. Business is less constrained than either government or organizations in the third sector but it is argued here that business should also have a clear purpose to fit the niche it occupies in the economy. Those who argue a different case, that the purpose of business is simply to make money for its shareholders, underplay the potential of business to be an agent for change and risk damage to both business and society.

For business, it is important to realize that its activities are integral to and inseparable from society; business delivers the products and services on which people rely, provides employment and acts as a home for people's long-term savings. The huge breadth and reach of business provides considerable power and influence over the direction of society, but generally this is not a power that is harnessed towards any higher purpose than for each business to succeed as best it can.

For society's savings, it is generally acknowledged that investing in equities is the best long-term investment because business is good at putting capital to work to earn a profit. This means that a large proportion of the investments held by pension funds and fund managers is held in equities. The owners of these investments (everyone) have, in theory, huge power over business but this is generally not exercised except to the extent of moving money around to where it will generate the highest return.

Business has huge latent power over society and society has huge dormant power over business but both parties have been persuaded to distance themselves from each other using the maxim of shareholder value. Instead of a direct control relationship between the owners and the corporation, shareholder value is used as the basis of the relationship. This concept is the bedrock of most finance modules on MBA programmes. Those going into management are taught to focus on delivering shareholder value; those who become investment managers are encouraged to focus on measures of shareholder value when deciding how to invest. Management focused on financial results and investors focused on financial return, pares away at the notion that there can be other objectives and other values.

This dysfunctional arrangement has set business on a disorganized frenzy of profit building to no better purpose than playing a slot machine. As corporations improve their ability to deliver shareholder value, they can become ever more divorced from society unless management spot the dangers and realise that shareholder value is a very narrow measure and must be used with caution.

To achieve sustained success, a business has to have a clearly defined role in society which is greater than the basic requirement to deliver a return to shareholders. It is a sad reflection on the current state of management thinking that it is necessary to restate this truism but without such foundations the corporation is bound to fail, sooner or later. The strategic process should support finding a place for the corporation that cements its place in society.

THE AGE OF RESPONSIBILITY

Governments have responsibility for the cohesion and success of the society to which they answer. They face some huge challenges ranging from climate change and the end of the era of fossil fuel to the problem of resource limits and creating jobs in an increasingly automated world. These problems require solutions and finding them is becoming urgent.

The current version of laissez-faire capitalism is not providing solutions; it is not even providing the possibility that there could be solutions. A system has arisen in which democratic governments are powerless to force through the degree of change required. Business may not be the cause of the problems but business is also not part of the solution, with little sign of systemic change to align business with the real needs of society.

Business has put its licence to operate at risk through behaviour which invites questioning the legitimacy of the model of corporate capitalism. Three examples will be used to illustrate the problem. These are not extreme examples of corporate wrongdoing, such as the massive fraud perpetrated by Enron executives revealed in 2001, but common-place examples of legal corporate behaviour. First under the responsibility spotlight are the tax affairs of the large multinational corporations Google and Starbucks. In 2013, it was reported widely in the media that these corporations had been using loopholes in tax law to manipulate their accounts to avoid paying tax in the UK. They defended their actions by claiming that they have a duty to maximize returns for their shareholders – to the maximum extent allowed by law. This corporate attitude challenges the government to close such loopholes and add yet more red tape. Gaming the tax system in this way leads to ever more complex rules and regulations providing a strait jacket for corporations in a wasteful merry-go-round of tax avoidance advisors against tax officials. This blatant tax avoidance by a Multinational Corporation (MNC) at the expense of the public purse is an unambiguous example where the case for more responsible behaviour is easy to understand. Other situations may not be so clear cut.

The second example is more nuanced and comes from the oil industry's strategic approach to the exploitation of unconventional oil. The context of the example is in a risky industry where accidents happen. The oil spill in the Gulf of Mexico in 2010 was the sort of accident which may have happened eventually drilling for oil pushed at the limits of technology in deep water. In this case, there were human errors and blame was laid on BP and its contractors. Every employee is fallible so mistakes will occur and there will be accidents, but what of the strategic decision to exploit unconventional oil such as the oil sands of Athabasca in Canada? This will involve not only environmental damage to excavate the oil sand but also energy-hungry processes required to separate the oil from the sand; unconventional oil is therefore a dirty high-carbon fuel compared with conventional oil. The pollution and environmental damage will not be an accident but a consequence of deliberate strategy. While society fails to deal with climate change and fossil fuel dependency, no law will have been broken. The question arises, should corporations exploit the inability of government to take action to close the fossil fuel economy or start to work with government on the challenges of closing it down? This example is typical of the dilemmas that corporations face.

The third example is Southern Cross, a provider of care homes for old people operating in the UK, which was acquired by the American private equity group Blackstone Capital Partners in 2004. This was the start of a buying spree in which Blackstone added Nursing Home Properties (NHP) the same year and Ashbourne Group care homes in 2005. By the end of 2005, Blackstone had built one of the largest portfolios of care homes in Britain financed mainly by debt (Sabbagh 2006). Blackstone reorganized the business under a sale-and-leaseback strategy placing the ownership of the properties in Nursing Home Properties (NHP). Blackstone then prepared NHP for sale as a property company and Southern Cross as a care home operating company. NHP was sold in 2006 for over £1.1 billion at a time when property investments were in demand and Southern Cross was floated on the stock market the same year. It is estimated that Blackstone banked a profit of up to £1bn on its investment (Ruddick 2011). However after the sale, Southern Cross was left with a debt burden and lease responsibilities which proved to be unsustainable in the wake of the 2008 financial crisis, leading to collapse in 2011. Blackstone argued strongly that they sold a sound business and it was the subsequent management of Southern Cross that caused its collapse (Blackstone 2011). Whoever was to blame, there was much concern among charities and the Government about the plight of Southern Cross's 31,000 residents caught in a game of corporate financial engineering. Anger was aimed at the company's former owner, private equity group Blackstone who did nothing illegal, but if this is the behaviour of the agents of capitalism there is no wonder that trust in business has evaporated.

These three examples show how business focussed solely on generating cash is not the way that corporations endear themselves to society and is not how they should fit into the fabric of society. Blatant tax avoidance, strategies that conflict with key government challenges and financial engineering at the expense of vulnerable stakeholders are not the methods of responsible corporate strategy.

The general view that has dominated policy for the last two decades is that free-market capitalism is to be defended, warts and all, for the benefits it brings. These three examples could be written off as unfortunate but ultimately small-scale failures but it is argued here that such examples are now common and show that blinkered adherence to market fundamentalism is no longer justifiable. The voices of dissent are expanding beyond anti-capitalist campaigners to include moderate people taking a sensible pragmatic view that if this is capitalism, it must be reformed (Tormey 2012). In the age of responsibility, government and society will demand that business finds a new sense of responsibility or the licence to operate will be withdrawn and replaced with a straitjacket of red tape squeezing the life out of the corporation.

THE EMERGING BUSINESS LANDSCAPE

The leaders of corporations are some of the most forceful, dynamic and ambitious people on the planet; they have to be to survive the heavy weight of expectation and conflicting pressures from many directions. Where this drive to succeed leads to irresponsible behaviour, this may force the hand of government to legislate. As their freedom to operate is restricted, business leaders will look for ways to break out and regain their freedom. The immediate, and ill-considered, reaction might be to lobby against regulation or ask consultants to identify new loopholes. Business leaders with foresight will anticipate the cycle of mutual distrust that such action is likely to initiate and take a different direction.

Recognizing the limitations of legislation sets the context to reboot the relationship between business and government. Corporate taxation is a good example where simplification is required to rescue the corporation from the complex mesh of regulations brought in by government officials in response to an army of highly paid consultants looking for loopholes. The alternative is a presumption that corporations pay a fair proportion of tax. Responsible businesses operating within the intended spirit of taxation will be safe from interference and save on expensive accountancy and tax advisor fees. Corporations that try to take whatever they can through exploiting weakness in the rules (simple straightforward tax rules will by their nature have the potential for loopholes) will risk getting sucked into expensive litigation and negative press coverage. Smart governments will craft tax regulation to make prosecutions easy but direct their officials to focus on corporations with a track record of attempting to manipulate the system. Businesses that fight against government intentions will be wasting resources that could be better employed while corporations with a solid record of compliance will retain the freedom to operate.

As both government and corporations appreciate the benefits of cooperation, the business landscape will change. In the place of an uneasy standoff, opportunities open up for each party to build on its strengths. Government has clear objectives but is weak in its ability to take action; while business is flexible in the objectives it adopts and very good at taking action. Government is risk averse and therefore can be timid; while business understands risk and can embrace risk where the potential return justifies it. The potential for synergy is enormous. For business to lead by embracing objectives that would normally be the realm of government can be a powerful strategic position to reinforce the corporation at the heart of society.

ALTERNATIVE STRATEGIC PHILOSOPHIES

Business can be extremely flexible in the markets it enters, the priorities set and how it operates. This flexibility is important to survival in a rapidly changing world. This book will provide a methodology to bring order to the complex process of crafting and comparing strategic alternatives. Before embarking on the detail, there are three high-level alternative strategic philosophies to choose between which are described here as 'Survival', 'Growth' and 'Prosperity'.

Survival

The philosophy of survival is a combative approach to the challenges of the business world. It is typified by focussing on selling more with ever increasing efficiency combined with cost cutting and finally, when the fight seems to be lost, drawing maximum cash out of the business before it folds. This Darwinian survival of the fittest is a very tough philosophy to follow which tends to arise from a lack of strategic thinking where the business is simply reacting to its environment. Such philosophy is depressingly common, and can be useful in circumstances when it is judged that a business has no future, but as a basis for the development of strategy it is the philosophy of failure.

Growth

The philosophy of growth involves an evolutionary approach searching out new opportunities through observing carefully the changing business landscape and anticipating future trends. It is typified by focussing on expansion into the markets with the most potential and developing products to keep up with fashion and changing customer preferences. This philosophy requires a robust strategic process based on careful analysis of current trends and the ability to respond quickly to have products or services available to exploit each new wave of opportunities. This approach has a solid heritage with a good record of success and intellectual support in the management literature as well as a staple of teaching in business schools.

Prosperity

The philosophy of prosperity requires redefining the corporation around driving change in society and the economy to create a space for the corporation to occupy. This requires a strategic process that goes beyond simple observation to understand the challenges that society faces, formulating possible solutions and set the corporation up as the prime delivery agent. Throughout corporate history there have been examples of businesses profiting from this approach ranging from the East India Company which thrived through the eighteenth and nineteenth centuries (Webster 2013) to Google today (Vise 2005). Modern management theory has tended to overlook the philosophy of prosperity because it is resource intensive and difficult. In the new era, where governments face some extraordinary challenges, this philosophy has the potential to reap huge rewards.

Each strategic philosophy has its uses. The philosophy of survival is, in effect, a static strategy (despite the frenetic behaviour of its managers) as no one has the time, space or spare resources to develop the business. This is appropriate for a business being used as a cash cow before being sold or closed down. The philosophy of growth is more useful, leading to responsive strategy embracing a willingness to change and adapt. This is likely to deliver consistent growth in share price measured over short reporting periods consistent with the expectations of shareholders with a short time horizon. The philosophy of prosperity has huge potential requiring thinking long-term and engaging with government and other agencies to work on solutions. This is likely to deliver the most sustainable returns over the long-term but needs patient investors and a strategy that allocates sufficient resources outside the current core business to explore and experiment with novel new business models.

CONCLUSION

Business operates under the umbrella of a licence provided by society. Over the last two decades many businesses and corporations have put this licence at risk, by losing sight of their role in society in a rush to deliver returns to investors. Rebuilding responsibility is required to rebuild trust and persuade government that business should be freed from regulations and interference. Strategy in the age of responsibility is considerably different to the narrow focus on bottom-line results that has come to dominate the strategic process. Corporations should retain their commercial focus but directed towards the challenges of this era. This is what society needs: a vibrant business sector empowered to establish sustainable and profitable enterprises free of government control and fit for the twenty-first century.

SUMMARY

- Laissez-faire capitalism is failing society, accelerating the pressure on the planet's finite resources and making it hard for governments to find a way beyond the era of fossil fuel. Force of circumstances will lead to government and society demanding that business finds a new sense of responsibility or its licence to operate will be withdrawn and replaced with a straitjacket of regulations.
- To achieve sustained success, a business has to have a clearly defined role in society over and above the basic requirement to deliver a return to shareholders.
- For business to lead by getting close to government can be a powerful strategic position to cement the corporation at the heart of society.
- Society needs business freed from governmental control and empowered to establish sustainable and profitable enterprises fit for the twenty-first century.

CHAPTER 2

TWENTY-FIRST-CENTURY OPPORTUNITIES

Business can step up to the challenge and thrive.

People have always worried about the problems of their current era, but humans have always muddled through in the end. It is human nature to wait to be forced and only then to act. The same will be true over the coming decades but there is an important difference. The current era is unique in that collectively we have the capability, for the first time in human history, to alter the planet in ways that would have consequences for thousands of years. Never before has humanity been so advanced, so capable and so able to transform its circumstances. It is unfortunate that our new abilities do not come with a renewal of our sense of collective responsibility. The same old muddling through, which has served us well enough up to now, has become a dangerous delusion. If business can break this delusion, the opportunities are immense. There have been many examples of 'cry wolf' as the environmental debate has heated up. Businesses expecting too much of government policy and persuaded to invest ahead of the curve may not generate the expected returns and get caught up in the froth of green investment with many apparently good ideas culled as commercial reality bites. As the transition to a more sustainable society gathers pace, business should focus on the opportunities with a sound business case – and the commercial logic is growing ever more persuasive. As political leaders start to understand the urgency, responsible corporations will be allowed considerable leeway to do what is necessary. This is a once-in-a-century opportunity to build profitable, respected and resilient corporations insulated from the erratic, often irrational, forces of the old twentieth-century capitalism. In this chapter a few key areas will be reviewed to give an outline of the scale and extent of the opportunities.

THE SUSTAINABLE REVOLUTION

A revolution in society and the economy is approaching as the world wakes up to the scale of the challenge of our era (McManners 2008; Stern 2010). The core challenge is how society and the economy will fare as easily-accessible resources run out. This challenge becomes hugely magnified as the majority of people finally and belatedly accept that there are environmental limits that should not be breached. This late conversion, after so much denial, will have wasted so much time that there will have to be revolutionary change. It is not a statement to make with any relish, but this works in business's favour, as in the struggle to regain stability politicians will be looking for agents that can get the job done.

On the down side, the Sustainable Revolution will bring disruption and uncertainties, causing grave difficulty for corporations which are slow to understand what is happening, and are left holding stranded assets as the revolution bites. On the up side, the opportunities will be almost boundless extending across industries and across sectors. A snap shot of some of the key opportunities is presented in the sections below as examples of the vast scope to engage with the required transformation of society and the economy.

As the forces of sustainability shape the strategic process, being different becomes easier. One constant unwavering requirement of the most successful business strategies is that, to be effective, strategy should be different. There is little to be gained from launching a me-too strategy which duplicates what another business can offer within the same market; that only leads to a destructive competition reducing profits for both parties. In a static world, finding a unique niche within the business landscape is exceedingly hard. In a world engulfed by revolution, where everything is in a state of flux, the variety of options is immense. The challenge becomes identifying which of the many commercial opportunities to pursue and working out how to craft strategy that can secure the corporation at the heart of its fulfilment.

It is logical to be optimistic that sustainability will become the basis of policy because everyone should want the continuation of civilization. Humans may procrastinate, vested interests may defend their position, but in the final analysis the cold logic that we have to live within the resources of the planet will win out, initiating complex, interconnected change (McManners 2009).

When the nature of the Sustainable Revolution is understood in board rooms, attitudes will shift from resistance to change and defence of the status quo to an attitude of 'bring it on'. The best strategic opportunities are those most needed by society and most difficult to deliver. This combination provides the possibility to establish uncontested space in which the corporation can thrive outside the cut-throat world of business-as-usual. A company that sits tight without embracing the new world order will become an also-ran.

The most pressing immediate challenge is fossil fuel:

THE DEMISE OF FOSSIL FUEL

Warnings of the end of oil have been heard so often that they are no longer heeded, even though it is an unavoidable fact that there is an end to oil – and it may be sooner than anyone supposes. The conventional view is that every last drop will be pumped out until reserves run out in around two or three decades from now. The rush to exploit shale gas has given succour to those who insist that the end of the fossil fuel economy may be even further off into the future, but the extent to which society will allow shale gas exploitation and whether the recoverable reserves match the hype is uncertain. Such developments in fossil fuel supplies can be used as an excuse to delay investment in alternatives, but the industry of extracting easy oil is already in decline. To maintain production, the industry will have to seek a licence from society to ramp up exploitation of the dirty sources such as oil shale and oil sand. If society does not grant such a licence the end of oil will come much sooner.

The approaching end of oil should be adequate justification for a massive investment programme in low-carbon technology but it is held back by those people and organizations gripped by short-termism. The issue that might break the stalemate is the small matter of climate change. Governments have been slow to move from rhetoric to action but the evidence that carbon dioxide emissions from fossil fuels are causing climate change (IPCC 2013), and that this could be a serious threat to human society, is now overwhelming. As more and more severe weather events such as droughts, floods and heat waves hit society and are attributed to the continuation of the fossil-fuel economy there will be a backlash against the politicians who have done so little for so long. The stage will be set for a crisis response; particularly if there are sustained droughts in two or more of the world's main food growing regions, sending world food prices through the roof.

The transition away from fossil-fuel to an economy running on renewable energy could have been a smooth transition if it had begun in the 1970s when the argument surfaced for reduced dependence on oil. Four decades would have been long enough to replace infrastructure and change manufacturing processes as part of a rolling replacement programme. That time has been squandered by the politicians (with the collusion of business) so the demise of the fossil-fuel economy will be an ill-planned lurch towards a low-carbon economy.

For corporations that are not prepared, this will be a serious threat; but for steadfast corporations that have planned for the end of oil it will be like holding a lottery ticket in a rigged lottery knowing the number is coming up, but not knowing when the ticket is to be drawn.

The end of the fossil-fuel economy will not be as anyone expects – even those who can see it coming. The degree of change is such that it defies detailed prediction as the market for energy is completely overturned. The current model is demand led; which means that as demand for energy rises investment flows into new power stations and oil production facilities on the assumption that fossil fuel reserves is not a limiting factor. The new energy market will be a supply-constrained market; which means as demand on limited renewable energy capacity increases the price rises. Excess energy demand drives prices higher forcing increased efficiency and supporting the business case for more renewable energy infrastructure but there is a time lag before the capacity can be built. In addition, although sun, wind and tide are free, there are limits to how much can realistically be harvested.

The new emerging energy market requires government action to smooth out what is certain to be a lumpy investment process. Governments will use taxation of fossil fuel on a rising and consistent basis to ensure that investment in renewable energy is viable. The current subsidy-based approach, attempting to hold energy prices at current levels while subsidizing renewable energy, will be abandoned

---

BOX 2.1 POLITICAL GRIDLOCK

- People accept higher energy prices caused by the rising market price of oil, even though the additional cash ends up in the coffers of the OPEC countries.
- People do not like higher energy prices caused by taxation by government, even though this keeps the tax receipts inside the economy for investment in low-carbon public infrastructure.
- The logical course of action is to drive fossil fuel prices high through taxation to drive adaptation in the economy by individuals and corporations and keep cash in the economy to support the government's responsibility to deliver low-carbon public infrastructure – but this is contrary to what people will easily accept.
- The logical course of action has the additional advantage that high taxation of fossil fuel will constrain demand and keep oil prices under control through the period of transition.
- Politicians are fearful of arguing for the logical course of action because they know high energy prices will be unpopular and they do not want the blame. This timidity leads to the pretence that the transition to a low-carbon economy can take place at current energy prices.
- The logic of high carbon taxes will win out in the end but in Western democracies this will happen only when there is majority support for switching to cleaner energy sources.
- The switch from holding energy prices steady to driving them higher through taxation could be fast because it needs only a change in policy and the argument is becoming increasingly persuasive.
- To break the political impasse, innovative politicians may reduce other taxes so the electorate experience a shifting tax burden rather than simply more taxation. Reducing consumption of fossil fuel is how individuals and corporations will keep their tax bills low which, of course, is the outcome required.

because it does not drive improved energy efficiency. The greenest energy is the energy that is no longer needed. Eventually the political process will accept that higher energy prices are integral to the low-carbon economy (Box 2.1).

Corporations that own renewable energy assets will see their profits rise in line with energy prices. When energy prices exceed the level required to pay off the capital investment, each further increase in energy price feeds directly through to the bottom line because the feedstock, such as sunshine, is free. These corporations will have to be patient waiting for the tipping point when their assets become super profitable. The market will be watching; as soon as high energy prices looks likely, the value of shares in these corporations will increase rapidly. The market's current view is that renewable-energy stocks are risky because they rely on government subsidies. These stocks are unloved by the markets because markets focus on the short-term, advised by investment analysts assuming governments will continue to avoid dealing with climate change. When the energy market switches direction, the need for increased renewable energy capacity is so great that the market will not be hit by overcapacity for decades into the future. Renewable energy assets will become gold-plated secure investments and be in great demand beyond the point when the fossil fuel economy starts to be wound down.

MANUFACTURING

The Sustainable Revolution will launch a renaissance in manufacturing. In Europe, and elsewhere, there are signs of change in response to increasingly stringent environmental regulations and recycling targets. It is becoming normal in industrial process and product design to consider the 'cradle-to-grave' lifecycle of products from initial manufacture through to end-of-life recycling. This seems like a major change as industry learns the new way of thinking but it is only the first stage of a more complex transformation.

The stage which is not yet widely understood, and which will overturn long-standing industrial norms is the adoption of 'cradle-to-cradle' manufacturing. This requires not only reconfiguring supply chains but also changing the nature of the relationship between manufacturer and consumer. In essence, in a resource-constrained world, products will be made, used, repaired and the material recovered to be incorporated in the next generation of product in a cycle that can be repeated almost indefinitely. The relationship between manufacturer and customer becomes very close and supply chains much shorter than now. The model of manufacturing in the Far East and shipped to Western markets before being junked will become obsolete. However, manufacturers have allowed their skills base to erode and consumers have been supplied with cheap throwaway products for so long that reverting to quality long-life products will seem like a major departure from current norms.

As cradle-to-cradle becomes the norm, there are changes which in today's retail market seem improbable. The sales process will evolve away from the sale of products to the provision of the service the product provides (McDonough and Braungart, 2002 and 2013). This seems very odd until you start to understand the significance of the new relationship between provider and customer. Instead of cars there will be personal mobility solutions; instead of washing machines there will be clothes washing facilities. The provider may choose to supply a car or a washing machine but it will be owned by the provider, maintained as required and replaced when it is cost-effective to do so. These generic service descriptions gives flexibility to the provider to offer the most effective and sustainable solution.

Corporations that lead the renaissance, and invest in sustainable design, will reap the rewards of bringing manufacturing closer to markets and earn a reputation for quality of products and services inherent in the cradle-to-cradle model. This shift will be in parallel with the rejection of the cheap-throwaway society by both government officials and customers. Corporations that resist the paradigm shift by continuing to make throw-away products will be exposed to increased government legislation and put their brand reputation at risk. In the new marketplace, a reputation for being 'cheap' can easily mutate into a reputation for being 'cheap and nasty'.

CITY INFRASTRUCTURE

The proportion of the people of the world living in cities is increasing and in 2008 passed 50 per cent. Therefore the evolution of cities is critically important to finding a sustainable future for humanity (Box 2.2).

BOX 2.2 CITIES FOR PEOPLE

Over the last 50 years, the developed world has built cities around the infrastructure required for cars; this is a design mistake which will take some decades and considerable investment to correct (McManners 2007). The characteristic of a sustainable city include:

- Compact design such that walking and cycling can be used for most local journeys.
- Good public transport such that car ownership is not a necessity.
- Cities as a tessellation of urban villages with a good range of local services.
- Quality public space provided to balance limitations on the size of private space to achieve the density required for sustainable transport solutions.
- Every roof put to use either for solar energy harvesting or urban agriculture.
- Low-carbon buildings designed to suit the local climate with a long-last core structure and fully recyclable fittings which can be replaced every 20 or 30 years.

It will take a major shift in attitude before sustainable city design enters the main stream. It will be very difficult for those responsible for the gleaming cities of the developed world, built around a network of freeways and jam-packed with cars, to accept that this affluent model is flawed. The shift in attitude may be beginning in Western countries (Dannenberg, Frumkin and Jackson 2011) but the opportunities to make it reality may be in the developing world (without legacy infrastructure) as policy makers try to avoid repeating the same mistakes. Architects and contractors who understand the new parameters of sustainable city design will win the work to build the cities of the developing world. An example is Masdar City in the United Arab Emirates which is being designed by UK-based Foster and Partners and engineering and environmental consultancy Mott MacDonald. The aspiration is to build the most sustainable city in the world. Through working on such projects construction companies can learn how to re-engineer Western cities as 'quality of life' becomes the prime design parameter.

For people residing in North America, the idea that cities could have fewer cars may seem impossible but that is only because urban design is focussed on the car such that cars become essential to everyday living. Focussing design on people leads to radically different urban structures. The challenge here is making a transition where everything has to change. In Europe, the challenge is more manageable as many cities have a compact design served well by public transport, but it will still require massive additional investment. In developing countries, the challenge is to understand that many of the cities, despite severe underperformance in sanitation and unreliable services, have arrived at potential models of sustainability through force of circumstance. It may be that the world's leading engineering corporations learn how to construct sustainable cities working in the relative freedom of cities starting with limited existing infrastructure.

This short section only scratches the surface but shows in brief outline that twenty-first-century cities will be different and the corporations that lead the transformation will reap the rewards.

TRANSPORT

Transport is a vital part of the economy and has a vital role in people's lives. This sector is particularly reliant on fossil fuel because the liquid fuels derived from oil are a perfect energy source for mobile applications. Such fuels have high energy density and are easily transported. Plans are discussed to decarbonize transport but each proposed solution has its drawbacks. The aviation industry claims it could run on biofuel but the quantities required are an order of magnitude greater than the likely available sustainable supply. Ground transportation could run on electricity, but the question is, how to generate enough electricity without fossil fuel. Ships could return to using wind as a source of propulsion but how could the tight deadlines of supply chain managers be met when progress depends on the vagaries of the wind.

The solution to sustainable transport is not to redesign each element but to redesign the whole system. Greener transportation is not just about low-carbon technology to replace existing transport options but about systemic change. Corporations focussed on single mode transport may miss the bigger picture and potentially miss valuable opportunities. Aviation is a prime example where effort is going into marginal change of each element while the overall business model remains unchanged. This can be understood because international agreements, airport design standards and the existing aircraft fleets are locked into the old twentieth-century model. There is a sustainable model for aviation but all these parameters need to change to make it reality including ramping up investment in rail as a credible alternative to short-haul flights (McManners 2012). Looking from outside the industry, it seems ridiculous that the transition to low-carbon aviation is stalled by the corporations inside the industry defending the status quo, but they have good reason to be fearful because many aviation businesses will not survive the shakeout.

Ground transportation will change through changes in society that make traveling less necessary coupled with increased use of electric propulsion. Rail operators will come to realise that their extensive real estate has the potential to host sufficient renewable energy harvesting to cover their energy needs and deliver a surplus (McManners 2012). Interestingly, serial entrepreneur Elon Musk, founder of Paypal has taken this concept further with a proposal for solar-powered ground transportation that completely changes what is understood to be a railway (Box 2.3). For cars, not only will there be an increase in the proportion of electric

---

BOX 2.3 HYPERLOOP – A WILD IDEA OR COMMERCIAL GOLD?

Elon Musk, CEO of Tesla motors and Space X has proposed a city-to-city elevated transit system that could take passengers and cars from Los Angeles to San Francisco in 30 minutes (Vance 2013). In Musk's vision, the 'Hyperloop' would transport people via aluminium pods enclosed inside steel tubes. These tubes would be mounted on columns 50 to 100 metres apart, and the pods inside would travel up to 800 miles per hour. The pods would be elevated on air bearings as air is pumped out of small holes in skis fitted to the bottom of the pods. The pods would be accelerated by linear electric motors powered by solar panels fitted atop the tubes. Excess energy would be stored in battery packs at each station, so the transport system could run 24-7.

There is little doubt that a system along these lines would be technically feasible; the question would be whether the business case would be commercially viable and in a low-carbon future this looks increasingly likely.

cars but the overall number of cars will decline as city design makes cars less of a necessity.

Sea transportation will return to using the wind that blows freely across the oceans supplemented by vast fold-out solar panels to use in light wind conditions. This will not be a reversion to ropes and canvas but use advanced aerodynamics supported by the latest control technology, and weather data from satellites. The management of sea transportation will be more complex but there are no technical barriers to implementing low-carbon sea transport; the barrier is a lack of business case while bunker fuel for ships is cheap and available without restriction. If this situation changes through policy decisions, the commercial dynamics for sea transportation could be overturned within a short space of time handing the corporations with plans for the transition a golden opportunity.

To tease out the opportunities in transport requires analysis that examines whole system solutions. This makes the analysis more difficult and more complex but exposes non-obvious strategic opportunities which are not apparent through the lens of business-as-usual.

AUTOMATION AND JOBS

It is deeply engrained in the business case for automation that machines are cheaper than people. Having being involved in making the case for large IT projects over the years, the savings in staff costs are almost always one foundation of the business case. As we enter the era when there is the technical ability to automate almost anything and everything, the government's problem of ensuring employment opportunities may become acute. It will become a valid exercise to look at the business case through the other end of the telescope. This section of this book is pushing at the boundaries of what hard-nosed business people will easily accept, but looking at the cost benefit analysis of employing more people to save on capital investment in robots and high-end computing becomes an interesting exercise, particularly where there are government incentives to recruit and retain people into the corporate family (McManners 2008).

THE EMERGING FUTURE

Joseph Schumpeter wrote about the creative destruction that capitalism can bring about as successive waves of technology replacing what has gone before (Schumpeter 1994). This is something to embrace as business leads the way into a resource-constrained low-carbon future. Energy market dynamics will flip to a new balance of demand drawing on renewable sources as fossil fuel is withdrawn. This will happen well before supplies are exhausted – the Stone Age did not end because the world ran out of stone. For transport, there is a golden age of advanced low-carbon technology waiting to be launched. For manufacturing, there is the prospect of a renaissance through taking resource efficiency to a new level. For urban design, a massive leap forward is feasible.

To exploit this new future, business has to get inside the thought processes that will bring it about. Businesses operating in sectors that will be destroyed should not wait to be wiped out but make strategic plans to extract maximum value to invest in ventures targeting the new opportunities. As investors understand the emerging future, it will become increasingly difficult to sell assets that have little or no role in the future industrial landscape; it makes commercial sense to move early to exit while there are still short-term returns to justify a valuation.

SUMMARY

- The Sustainable Revolution is approaching, bringing with it immense opportunities to build profitable, respected and resilient corporations as the world wakes up to the scale of the challenge of reaching the limit of easily-accessible resources combined with the knowledge that climate change is a serious threat to society.
- The best strategic opportunities are those most needed by society and most difficult to deliver. This combination provides the possibility to establish uncontested space in which the corporation can thrive outside the cut-throat world of business-as-usual.
- The range of opportunities is immense from renewable energy and low-carbon transport to a renaissance in manufacturing and the redesign of cities and their infrastructure – and more.
- Corporations that lead the Sustainable Revolution will reap the rewards; the corporations slow to understand the new economy will struggle.

CHAPTER 3

BEYOND GLOBALIZATION

There are limits to growth.

(Meadows 1972 and 2004)

Economic globalization[1] is the increasing economic interdependence of national economies across the world through a rapid increase in cross-border movement of goods, service, technology, and capital (Joshi 2009). The recent era of globalization has been a 'rising tide that lifts all boats'[2] but it is reaching the high water mark. It has been exceedingly good for the bottom line of global corporations, but as resource limits are reached and growth falters organizations that do not have a resilient strategy, to move with the tide of change, will be left beached as the tide goes out.

The future of globalization could take two directions. First, there could be deeper integration and extended free markets brought about by continuing with a narrow focus on economic outcomes. Second, there could be a shift to a global economy with different characteristics through adopting the emerging policy framework of proximization (explained later in this chapter) where governments find they must shift focus towards sustainable policy and secure access to key resources. These two alternative directions have significantly different strategic implications. The former is an extrapolation of the macroeconomic policy of the last 25 years and could be described as 'business as usual'. The latter is a major shift away from the status quo, and has yet to gain strong support, but shifting in this direction is inevitable if sustainability becomes the bedrock of policy.

Understanding the basis of the approaching shift in macroeconomics is the foundation to engaging corporate strategy with the changing economic picture.

---

1   Globalization has come to mean many things in different contexts but in this chapter the focus is on macroeconomic policy with 'globalization' synonymous with 'economic globalization'.

2   A phrase coined by Ted Sorensen (2008), advisor to American President JF Kennedy, applied here to free-market policies, and the subsequent trade which should theoretically increase incomes for all participants.

In this short chapter, the changing macroeconomic parameters are covered in sufficient detail to support the detailed analysis of changing economic priorities presented in the next chapter (Chapter 4).

THE RISE OF ECONOMIC GLOBALIZATION

Economic globalization has accelerated over the last quarter century largely as a consequence of the macroeconomic policies pursued by the US, the UK and others; and championed by the IMF and the World Bank. The 'standard' reform package, which became known as the Washington Consensus, encompassed policies such as opening with respect to both international trade and investment, and the expansion of market forces within the economy (Serra et al. 2008).

Economic globalization has had a profound impact on multi-national corporations (MNCs), opening up markets and allowing economies of scale built on super-efficient extended global supply chains. Chief executives and policy makers have in effect been working to a shared agenda improving bottom-line performance for global corporations and delivering growth in GDP as sought by the politicians.

This period of extraordinary global economic growth (until the economic crisis of 2008) coincided with a massive increase in the demand for resources and rising carbon dioxide emissions. The headline figures for economic growth masked other problems such as job losses in manufacturing in the developed economies and increased pressure on the environment in developing countries as polluting industries relocated from the rich countries, where environmental regulations were being tightened, to countries with weaker controls and a lower cost base. Policies in support of economic globalization have been the logical consequence of focussing on the objective of increasing GDP. As politicians and their advisors start to look at wider measures of success they will no longer give unswerving support to the Washington Consensus policies opening the way to the consideration of other macroeconomic policy options.

GLOBALIZATION HAS PEAKED

The financial crisis of 2008 was the first tangible sign that the policies of economic globalization have a limited lifespan. There is now growing dissatisfaction with the current economic paradigm with a growing body of evidence that the twenty-first century needs a new approach to economic management (Cowling and Tomlinson 2011; Stiglitz 2010). What that new approach might comprise is one of the challenges in economics today.

There is a quandary in global economic and political circles as to what to do about globalization. Do the evident problems require more globalization or less? The advocates of increased globalization see the associated problems as examples of weak implementation to be solved through yet further openness and deeper integration. This approach has intellectual appeal and is 'politically correct' but relies on effective global environmental agreements and willingness for countries to share out the world's resources on an equitable basis. Such ideas are based on good intentions but take little account of real-world constraints. The desirability of fixing globalization keeps world politicians from considering the possibility that the economic framework of globalization might be flawed. This is unfortunate because this is slowing the debate about alternatives. Eventually it can be expected that realism takes over as pragmatists come to the fore who accept that it is unrealistic to expect much of the UN-brokered global agreements opening the way to national governments to lead action which will inevitably focus on defending their interests. An imperfect solution arrived at through countries taking the lead in their own national interest is likely to be preferable to a theoretical solution that is always pushed off into some long-distant future.

The hangover from the 2008 financial crisis refused to go away in the years that followed, because the cure attempted was more of the same, rather than reform to macroeconomic policy. Like drunkards who cannot see the error of their ways, it takes time for policy makers to accept that the time has come to get off the globalization bandwagon. The imperative to move sustainability up the policy agenda could lead to intense pressure for reform of macroeconomic policies but only when there is a credible alternative.

AN ALTERNATIVE POLICY FRAMEWORK – 'PROXIMIZATION'

A credible alternative to the policies of economic globalization has yet to be accepted as the new standard of macroeconomics. Economist in the leading economies, with the backing of politicians, continue to try to fix globalization including some articulate outspoken critics such as Joseph Stiglitz (2010), but corporations cannot afford to wait and see what emerges from this rearguard action. Global corporations have been actively engaged in shaping economic globalization – and have profited from being at the heart of its growth. Global corporations can also profit from being at the centre of the next chapter of evolving economic policy. The detail has yet to be defined so business can engage in the debate to ensure that what is good for society is good for the corporation.

The new macroeconomics presented here is 'Proximization' defined as (McManners 2008 and 2010):

> *Proximization is selfish determination to build sustainable societies, aimed at social provision and driven by economic policy, whilst minimizing adverse impacts on the environment.*

The proximization framework emerges as national governments take back control to provide the stable macroeconomic context within which countries can manage their affairs including securing supplies of resources and fulfilling their responsibilities to their citizens for environmental integrity, social cohesion and economic well-being. The modifications impact on every area of policy because to change anything requires everything to change. Steering the current highly complex global economy into this new reality, without the luxury of isolated incremental change, means that the world is approaching a tipping point. This will not be a neatly orchestrated change of policy but a disorganized scramble as countries secure their future prosperity.

IMPLICATIONS FOR BUSINESS EXECUTIVES

This juncture in world affairs is full of uncertainty. Business can sit on the side-lines and await developments or engage with anticipating and shaping the new economic reality. There are many economists, politicians and business leaders who are yet to be persuaded that the policies of globalization should change, let alone that the changes will look like the policy framework presented here. It would therefore be sensible not to accept this analysis as an accurate prediction but to expect that reality could veer off in a number of directions. Some corporations, such as the oil company Shell, are analysing the future possibilities through scenarios (Shell 2013) but no one has a crystal ball to know the outcome.

The strategic implications of the new macro-economic framework will be significant. The assumption that there will be continued expansion of economic globalization is deeply rooted in many corporate strategies – it is easier to assume maintenance of the existing state of affairs. As political leaders, government officials and business CEOs discuss how to fix the broken world economy they are like military commanders discussing their experiences from the last war instead of thinking through how to fight the next. They discuss increasing the resilience of global supply chains instead of reconfiguring them; they continue to look for global synergies in manufacturing instead of nurturing national business units anticipating the shift to manufacturing closer to markets; and the switch to low-carbon technologies is seen as something off in the future after the global economy has recovered rather than an integral part of rebuilding the new economy.

Military commanders discover that they have to fight the war they find, not the war they want, and scrabble to quickly change tactics and have the arms industry make the new equipment. History is littered with contrary military thinkers who came to the fore and were catapulted into senior positions pushing the old guard aside, such as Admiral Lord Nelson (1805) at the Battle of Trafalgar, Field Marshall Montgomery in North Africa (1942–43) and Major General David Petraeus in the Iraq War (2003–04). The same will happen in today's corporations where the people who read and heed this book will find it hard to be heard but by speaking out will ensure their careers are loaded into the corporate catapult ready to be thrust into the senior roles when the crisis hits. It will be a matter of personal choice how far and how fast this new thinking permeates the corporate hierarchy. Astute and ambitious executives involved in strategy may hedge their bets by being a step ahead of their colleagues by proposing strategy that is a sound launching pad for operating in the new economy but which does not bet the future of the corporation (or their careers) on a particular timeline.

CONCLUSION

The continuation of business-as-usual is deeply engrained in world economic policy, so strategy has to be able to work within the current macroeconomic framework. However, globalization has (probably) run its course. A new paradigm has yet to bed in but the general parameters are emerging. There will be a time lag before formal macroeconomic policy reflects the emerging new reality but business does not have to wait to see how the future pans out. Corporations can, and should, engage with shaping the future beyond globalization and crafting strategy to exploit the new world economic order. The pressure for change is building and when change comes it could be rapid as it is finally accepted that macroeconomic policy has to change. It may be premature to turn away from business-as-usual, and bet the future of the corporation on proximization taking hold, but a strategy that does not factor in the future beyond globalization will be vulnerable when the switch in macroeconomic priorities occurs.

SUMMARY

- There is a growing body of evidence that the twenty-first century needs a new approach to economic management; what that new approach might comprise is one of the challenges in economics today. There are signs that some corporations are starting to consider the possibility of fundamental change but advocates of maintaining the status quo still dominate business and politics.
- The world is approaching a tipping point. This will not be a neatly orchestrated change of policy but a disorganized scramble as national governments take back control to provide the stable macroeconomic context within which countries can manage their affairs including securing supplies of resources and fulfilling their responsibilities to their citizens for environmental integrity, social cohesion and economic well-being.
- The pressure for change is building and when change comes it could be rapid as it is finally accepted that macroeconomic policy has to change. A strategy that does not factor in the future beyond globalization will be vulnerable when the switch in macroeconomic priorities occurs.

CHAPTER 4

CHANGING ECONOMIC PRIORITIES

The challenge for corporations is to understand the changing economic priorities, to configure the business to thrive through a period when policy objectives emerge that require deep-rooted change.

Current macroeconomic policies have their roots back in the twentieth century and have held sway for nearly three decades but change is now overdue. When the world economy was set on its current course, Ronald Reagan was in the White House and Margaret Thatcher in 10 Downing Street; they championed free trade and open markets in the belief that this was the best economic policy for their era. However these macroeconomic policies have had damaging side-effects so, as is always the case, economic policy will change to fit the current set of challenges. Anticipating the shape and dynamics of the twenty-first century global economy gives corporate planners the chance to be a step ahead of the politicians. Global corporations were active participants in, and at times architects of, the globalized economy. Forward-looking MNCs should now be working out how to shape the corporation and its activities to fit the evolving new macroeconomic framework.

Economic analysis is at the heart of every policy decision by government and every commercial decision by business. The assumption that the economic rationale rules policy seems to be unassailable but the time has come to reassess the role of economics. Human society, and the people that comprise it, do not behave as rationale economic machines – as marketing executives know. Through advertizing and brand management people can be persuaded to spend in economically inefficient ways. This marketing notion, that the raw economic argument can be overruled, may migrate from corporations, trying to sell to consumers, to policy makers responsible for crafting balanced policy. The priorities of economic policy will change as economic analysis is brought back to its true purpose to facilitate other policies rather than an incestuous aim in itself.

In this chapter, an insight is provided into the changing economic parameters of the twenty-first century; in particular 'energy', 'commodities' and 'trade'. These areas are chosen for analysis because here the conventional economic logic will be overturned in favour of higher policy objectives. The logical analysis presented here should not be taken as a precise template because the pressure for change will meet irrational resistance. It could also be a mistake to assume that people will embrace sustainable economic policy, but the logic of sustainability is so strong that it is likely to win out in the end after a number of policy reversals and dead ends.

THE STATE OF THE ECONOMY

GDP is deeply engrained as the prime measure of the economy and used as a proxy for progress. Efforts to develop alternative measures, such as the UN's Human Development Index, are slow to materialize but just as corporations should be wary of a narrow focus on the bottom line, so governments will become increasingly wary of relying on GDP. There is little sign yet that economic policy will shift ground to embrace 'quality of life' above GDP but when it happens it will provide part of the context for changing economic priorities.

Meanwhile, for business, the general state of the economy is a strategic factor constraining the viability of commercial options. At times of economic stability, corporations vie for business in a transparent market where everyone knows the parameters. When the economic parameters change, the relative merits of strategic options also changes, affecting the viability of previously successful lines of business but also providing opportunities for new business models and new products or services, or old products provided in different ways. When the degree of change is such that it goes much further and overturns the old economic parameters, a free-for-all can ensue where nimble corporations can reap huge rewards. The flip side is that corporations with large investments in the current industry may be wiped out.

Extrapolating past trends is common in economic analysis but this method will no longer be a sound guide as governments exert their authority to use economic methods to implement sustainable policy.

A case study of building construction is carried through this chapter to illustrate the degree of change. Those working in the construction industry will know that the situation is far more complex than shown here, but this simplified view serves well enough as an example of the general case of shifting priorities. In each sector of the economy, the consequences of the changing economic parameters will vary between industries and localities as the old certainties are removed. A brief snap shot of the current situation in building construction is shown in Box 4.1.

BOX 4.1 BUILDING CONSTRUCTION (1)

- Construction is a major sector of the economy which is highly sensitive to overall economic conditions and used by government as a barometer of economic health.
- Recent fashion has been for international designs to be adopted (although particular construction techniques depend on local levels of expertise).
- The higher value construction components are sourced from the global market based on least cost.
- Concrete is the structural material of choice being strong, easily automated and flexible in how it is deployed.
- Heating or cooling is provided by bolt-on plant and equipment as required.

ENERGY MARKETS

The price of energy has been linked to the price of fossil fuel for as long as anyone alive can remember. The price is a combination of the cost of extraction and rent to whoever controls access to the deposits. The modern oil industry started in the United States in the nineteenth century where each new strike brought more capacity to the market risking undermining the price. The oil industry actively encouraged more consumption to retain profitability in the market (Yergin 1991). This was a rationale economic response to the challenges of the time even though in hindsight it can be seen how this set up a culture of gas-guzzling cars and high consumption which endures today when the circumstances are very different. This is a good example of an excessively narrow economic focus leading to inappropriate outcomes; those influencing the evolution of the new energy market should take note.

The oil market is now mature with high demand matched by high production, with organizations like OPEC (Organization of Petroleum Exporting Countries) seeking to ensure a stable market. OPEC will try to defend their income streams from oil for as long as possible but the situation will soon start to look untenable. The current worry is that supply may no longer be able to match increased demand so that prices could rise exponentially. This blinkered view underplays the significance of the approaching shift in energy markets. If governments could find the foresight, courage and political backing they could drive the transition without a huge spike in the oil price. In fact, it would be theoretically possible to return the market to a position of oversupply encountered in nineteenth-century United States but only when governments make the decisive switch away from oil.

It seems politically impossible to win the argument that society should run on energy sources other than fossil fuel, but the transition has to take place eventually and technically it can be done. One way or another fossil fuel has to be withdrawn from the economy. As the current economy is based on fossil fuel this means completely re-engineering the economy. The economic parameters are not simply shifted but reset to a different basis.

The prime energy sources for the new economy are all forms of renewable energy. The key economic issue is that energy will be more expensive. The cost of harvesting renewable energy is higher than the cost of extracting fossil fuel and the available capacity is limited by factors such as the total area of roof available for solar panels and the extent to which people are prepared to allow wind turbines to cover the landscape. The positive economic aspect is that much more of the rent element, instead of going into the exchequer of the oil-rich nations, stays within national and local economies.

Current levels of energy demand, drawing only on renewable capacity, would send energy prices sky high (giving a huge bonus to those who own renewable energy assets) and provide a strong incentive to save energy through efficiency measures. The current approach of keeping energy prices at current levels and subsidizing renewable energy does not engage investment in low-energy solutions. The future energy market will settle into a new balance of investment in renewable energy infrastructure and ultra-efficient energy use. The technology exists now to build such radically different infrastructure; all it requires is a shift in economic priorities.

As transport migrates to alternative fuels, transport will get more expensive changing the commercial dynamics of supply chains, altering affordable commuter profiles and changing city design parameters. Manufacturing processes will change to use much less energy and products with high embodied energy will become expensive or be replaced by alternatives. Every part of the connected economy is reconfigured as high energy prices ripple through stripping out the old and making a business case to support investment in the new.

The switched energy market will have a profound effect on our example of the building construction sector (Box 4.2).

The end point, after withdrawal of fossil fuel and after the economy has been reconfigured, is a better economy (in many ways) but the degree of change and disruption is far greater than any politician will admit. It is possible that democratic procrastination will lead to collapse of the current economy as a staging point on the journey but whether the journey is smooth or difficult it is a journey that must be embarked upon. Business can help itself, and help society, by starting the journey in advance of the politicians finding their resolve.

BOX 4.2 BUILDING CONSTRUCTION (2)

- High energy prices overturn the previous economic model for construction.
- City design shifts towards living and working places in closer proximity.
- The infrastructure requirements for remote working influences house and office design.
- The required technical changes are feasible but industry norms are radically different.
- High levels of insulation are required including, for example, triple-glazed windows which are common in cold regions and will become the norm across all markets.
- Increased preference for local supply as cost of transportation is high.
- The need for heating or cooling is dramatically reduced through good design and the first choice of energy supply is renewable energy harvested from all roof areas.
- Industry has to learn new skills throughout the trades to be able to design and build low-energy buildings.

COMMODITY MARKETS

Open world markets have kept the price of commodities low while there are ample supplies but as resource limits are reached prices will escalate. Already the production of commodities like copper has exhausted the highest grade ores and has started to exploit low-grade deposits of as little as 0.2% concentration (Martensen 2011). Such low-grade ores require considerable processing which is energy intensive, so rising energy prices will amplify commodity price rises. Another example is the production of cement which is also energy-intensive so cement prices will rise. Countries will be forced to turn their back on open markets and focus on securing access to continuation of supply. There will be huge commercial pressure to implement a circular economy in which virgin commodity inputs are replaced as far as possible by material reuse. Some changes to our example of the building construction sector are shown in Box 4.3.

BOX 4.3 BUILDING CONSTRUCTION (3)

- High commodity prices overturn previous economic model for construction.
- Construction components will be built to last or easy to recycle to make the most efficient use of construction material. The core structure will be designed to last for a hundred years with other components recyclable/biodegradable and replaced every 20–30 years.
- Materials produced through energy-intensive manufacturing such as cement will be expensive, making concrete less affordable leading to resurgence in other construction techniques such as stonemasonry requiring a larger skilled workforce.
- Industry has to learn a new skills set throughout the trades to be able to design and build with maximum efficiency of resource throughputs.

TRADE

Trade is a vital aspect of the macroeconomic framework. Over a number of decades the focus has been expansion with the aim of increasing economic growth with the World Trade Organization (WTO) acting as ringmaster. This approach will no longer be appropriate as the world enters the era of diminishing resources. The focus of trade policy will shift to securing supplies and ensuring the sustainability of economies. Instead of encouraging competition between economies based purely on cost, the future will be the exchange of commodities, goods and services to secure access to key resources.

Free-trade areas are likely to be less open to outsiders with rules and regulations to retain key resources inside the trading bloc. There may also be trade corridors based on bilateral arrangements to establish secure sustainable resource flows between particular economies with complementary needs. The WTO will need to change or be side-lined as governments act to protect their prime interests.

As governments take action to protect their interests, corporations will need to be engaged locally orchestrating networks of largely autonomous national businesses in a world of much less transportation and circular resource flows. Brands, knowledge and key components will be managed globally but bulk manufacturing and service delivery will be local businesses. Some changes to the example of the building construction sector are shown in Box 4.4.

BOX 4.4 BUILDING CONSTRUCTION (4)

- Countries become more self-sufficient due to resource restrictions and high transport costs.
- Building design becomes highly specific to the locality, climate and local resource availability.
- Innovation in construction will focus on being in tune with local conditions in ways that are both resource efficient and low-energy.
- Buildings will be healthier as they make maximum use of natural ventilation and design that maximizes solar gain or solar screening as required by the locality.
- Detailed design will use in-depth knowledge of local conditions and use locally sourced construction components while leveraging maximum advantage from global research and development into advanced building technologies.
- Industry has to learn a new skills set throughout the trades to be able to design and build low energy buildings with maximum efficiency of resource throughputs and tuned precisely to local conditions.

CONCLUSION

Economic policy is in a state of flux where the old rules of thumb will soon no longer apply. There are step changes in economic priorities coming through as policy makers bring economic policy back under control and in support of higher objectives. Focussing on economic outcomes and the bottom-line is like focussing on keeping a car in good repair and driving such that it does not hit the curbs. This might be fundamental to completing the journey but the bigger strategic issue is which road you are on. Governments and corporations should look through what is a dirty windscreen into the future to anticipate the next bend in the road and be open-minded as to where the best route through the issues and challenges will lead.

The challenge for corporations is to understand the changing economic priorities, to configure the business to thrive through a period when policy objectives emerge that require deep-rooted change.

SUMMARY

- To understand, in outline, the parameters of the new emerging economy, brings clarity to strategic thinking and provides one part of the foundation on which to build resilient strategy.
- The current economic framework is based on fossil fuel; to withdraw fossil fuel requires high energy prices to ripple through the economy stripping out the old and supporting the business case for investment in the new low-energy infrastructure.
- Open world markets have kept the price of commodities low while there are ample supplies but as resource limits are reached there will be huge commercial pressure to implement a circular economy in which virgin commodity inputs are largely replaced by material reuse.
- Governments are likely to back off from the policies of free trade to securing supplies and ensuring the sustainability of their economies; corporations will need to adapt to the new reality.

CHAPTER 5

THE PURPOSE OF THE CORPORATION

'...shareholder value is the dumbest idea in the world. Shareholder value is a result, not a strategy.' Jack Welch, 2009

Before embarking on a strategic appraisal, there is an important question, so obvious that it is easily overlooked. What is the purpose of the corporation? This is fundamental because corporations with a strong sense of core purpose are more likely to survive and prosper over the long-term. As the winds of change blow through society and the economy the corporation may be buffeted but not blown off course. Such deep-rooted corporate commitment is also a defence against the fads that blow through the corridors of business schools. One particular and damaging approach, which gained a strong following, is the concept of strategy designed to deliver shareholder value. Corporations should re-examine their core purpose, not to deliver shareholder value, but to find and define their place within society and the economy. There are close parallels with governments as they decide their programme, not to deliver a balanced budget, but to find and define a programme that delivers the policy and a portfolio of services that society needs. A balanced budget is of course a fundamental attribute of good government policy; but is not the objective. Delivering shareholder value is a fundamental attribute of sound corporate strategy; but should not be the prime objective.

SHAREHOLDER VALUE

Shareholder value has been elevated to a place in modern management theory that outweighs its worth (Stout 2012). It does not deserve a section in this book on strategy except to debunk it and take it out of the strategic equation. Corporations make money for shareholders, of course, but this should be part of much wider responsibilities. Focussing on shareholder value has been one of the dimmest ideas ever introduced, encouraging executives to focus on manipulating the figures to satisfy the short time horizon of investment managers. Corporations require a purpose that meshes with the needs of society cementing the corporation at the foundations of a sustainable and resilient economy; shareholder value does little to support this purpose.

The father figure of Shareholder Value Jack Welch, Chief Executive General Electric (1981–2001) encapsulates the current view of its utility in an interview with the *Financial Times* (Guerrera 2009):

> *The idea that shareholder value is a strategy is insane.*

In *Fixing the Game*, Roger Martin (2011) argues that American capitalism is in a sorry state because of a commitment to the idea that the purpose of the firm is to maximize shareholder value. This theory has led to a naive and wrong-headed linking of the real market – the business of designing, making, and selling products and services, with the expectations market – the business of trading stocks, options, and complex derivatives. Martin shows how this tight coupling has been engineered with a massive growth in stock-based compensation for executives and a single-minded focus on the expectations market. This is not only plain wrong, but Martin argues that this approach will drive the economy from crisis to crisis unless the situation is fixed.

Martin traces the trouble back to 1976 when finance professor Michael Jensen and Dean William Meckling of the Simon School of Business at the University of Rochester published a paper in the *Journal of Financial Economics* entitled 'Theory of the Firm: Managerial Behaviour, Agency Costs and Ownership Structure'. This seemingly innocuous paper tackled the principal-agent problem which occurs, the article argued, because agents have an inherent incentive to optimize activities and resources for themselves rather than for the owners. Jensen and Meckling's (1976) solution to such irresponsible management behaviour was to propose that the singular goal of a company should be to maximize the return to shareholders. Looked at from a narrow financial perspective, in the context of the problem being addressed, it was a logical argument, but their fix for irresponsible behaviour has encouraged management to ignore the long-term future of the corporation and shift such irresponsible behaviour towards ensuring that shareholders get the maximum return. There is an interesting parallel with discovering that the management are running a scam; it is obvious that the management should be disciplined or sacked; to insist that the scam is extended and formalized so that shareholders get their share of the take would be scandalous.

It is patently right that the executives of a corporation should not manage the corporation to line their own pockets but it is no better to manage the corporation to maximize short-term returns to current shareholders. Both these approaches are dead ends leading to management focussing on manipulating the financial figures rather than focussing on the real business. It is fundamental to responsible management to behave for the good of the corporation. The corporation is much more than its executives and much more than its current shareholders. Of course investors expect a return on their investment but this is a by-product of running a successful corporation. Shareholder value is at best a distraction and at worst a dangerous delusion and should have no more than a minor role in strategic change, or no role at all if you make the assumption that responsibility to shareholders and other stakeholders is a fundamental non-negotiable foundation to management analysis.

THE DECLARATION OF PURPOSE

A business run by an entrepreneur or small management team can operate without a specific statement of purpose. Such small teams can, in effect, make it up as they go along; reinforcing success and cutting losses on lines of business that prove not to be profitable. They should however be looking for a core purpose if they aspire to become a large sustainable business. For the larger corporation, with a head office consisting of multiple departments and operations split over many business units, a clear statement of purpose is vital. This ensures that all staff pull in the same direction, investors understand what they have invested in and customers know the nature of the club they join when they buy the product or service.

The statement of purpose is at a higher level than the specific product, process or service, these being tactical responses to fulfilling the purpose. For example, the UK corporation, Riversimple designs and builds hydrogen fuel-cell cars but it does not define its core purpose as building cars. Riversimple defines its purpose as:

> To systematically pursue the elimination of the environmental impact of personal transport. (Riversimple 2013)

This statement does not tie the company into building and selling cars but gives the firm the freedom to think laterally to examine the total process model of personal mobility (currently served by selling cars) and consider where the business can make its future.

The few words that comprise the statement of purpose may be the most valuable words that come out of the strategic analysis. The strategic process needs freedom from constraints but the corporation's day-to-day activities need unwavering clear direction. It is useful to consider the statement of purpose right at the start of the strategic process but it should be open to negotiation until the strategy is finalized. The agreed statement of purpose should encapsulate a vision that can be shared by everyone close to the business.

SETTING DIRECTION

Teasing out the purpose of the corporation is not about defining where it is now, but where it is going. It may be that the corporation already has a clear purpose, which remains appropriate, but it needs to be tested and challenged. Four questions about the purpose of the corporation are useful to draw out some fundamental thinking:

1. Is this something that is needed?
2. Is this something special?
3. Is this something that is enduring?
4. Is this something wanted?

Needed

The corporation should be in the business of satisfying a real need. For some businesses, such as those providing food, water or power there is a clear need, as there is for services such as insurance and banking; but for some corporations this question can lead to interesting further analysis. If the answer indicates that the corporation is selling a product or service for which there is no real need there is a danger that as consumerism loses its hold on society the corporation will vaporize. The 'need' could be something intangible such as making people feel good but recognizing this as the need being satisfied is important to opening the strategic analysis to a wide variety of options. There are also needs that are outside society but still real, such as the need to conserve the eco services of the planet. This is a clear need but becomes valuable only when society demands action. If society cares little about the planet there will not be a business opportunity to exploit. However, discovering that the need the corporation satisfies is to simply making people feel good, could lead to adding a tangible need through engaging people with saving the planet. This may not be important now but there is every chance that a real need such as this will rise up higher in people's priorities sooner or later. The corporations that have grown large on consumerism, peddling trinkets and branded trifles, could transform themselves into saviours of the planet[1]. This is one example; the general point is to identify the tangible and intangible needs that the corporations is seeking to satisfy because without this the corporation is only a money-making machine – and money-making machines are prone to failure.

Special

The corporation should ideally be doing something unique and difficult to replicate, to be able to carve out an uncontested space to operate. It may be doing one thing to an exceptionally high standard that others cannot match or operating a complex network each part of which is replicable but adds up to corporate machine of unrivalled capability. Uniqueness does not need to be absolute but

---

1   To make strategic sense this would have to be a genuine change at the heart of the corporation or the accusations of 'green wash' could be far more damaging than doing nothing.

can be relative to the market served. For example, a successful business model in one market can be rolled out as the template for another market. Corporations therefore have to move quickly to migrate successful business models to new markets because it is fair game for the incumbent local corporations to observe, copy and deploy a similar business model. Copying the same business model in the same market is best avoided as it initiates a price-based competition which can detrimental to both commercial parties. Competing on cost is one of the strategies to deploy (discussed later) but it is a weak starting point in defining the core purpose of the corporation. The requirement to be 'special' means being different to competitors and is a fundamental attribute of most successful strategies.

Enduring

The basis of long-term success is to find an enduring need to satisfy in a unique way. Reaping the rewards of exploiting a series of fleeting opportunities is the nature of business in fast-moving markets such as Telecoms, but underlying these skirmishes there should be a master plan based on an enduring need and an enduring strategy to exploit that need. For example, the need to communicate is an enduring need and delivering ergonomic communication capabilities that are intuitive to use is an enduring strategic position that sits above the rapidly changing technological landscape. Nokia had an unassailable strategic position for over a decade based on mobile phones with a complex supply chain second to none. Its undoing was realizing too late that the mobile phone would be replaced by more generic communication devices. Making mobile phones turns out not to be an enduring strategic position. Focussing on a particular product can be more efficient and maximize short-term returns but is vulnerable over the longer term. Satisfying an enduring need with an enduring strategic position is a defence against being caught out by shifting markets and evolving technology.

Wanted

A corporate direction that is needed, special and enduring will not be commercially viable unless it is wanted by both customers and investors. A simple view of strategy may recommend looking for a niche that customers want and where investors are keen to invest (Campbell et al. 2002). However care is needed because this is the thinking that leads to stock market bubbles like the dot-com boom of 1998–2000 (Lowenstein 2004). It was perceived that customers would want the new on-line services and investors wanted to invest in companies planning to supply. This focus on 'want' expanded rapidly out of control only to collapse as reality returned. It may seem counterintuitive but the 'want' factor should not be driving strategic direction. Whether customers want the product or service is important tactically but at the strategic level the issue is whether the corporation can persuade customers to buy. The same is true for investors; the issue is not what investors want, but can the corporation persuade investors to invest. A strategic direction which is special, needed and potentially enduring but not wanted by customers or investors has huge locked-in value. The corporation has the time and space to develop the key capabilities and lodge patents flying under the radar of competitors. When the time is right this value can be unlocked by selling the concept to investors and engaging customers through marketing. It will be like pushing at an open door if this is something that satisfies a real need.

STEADFAST OR EVOLVING?

Throughout the process of strategic analysis, the purpose of the corporation is open to debate but at the end of the process there should be an agreed statement of purpose. Any proposal that comes to the board for approval has to conform to the strategy in accordance with the purpose of the corporation. Allowing the purpose to bend with circumstances can lead to drift unless the change is as a result of a new in-depth strategic appraisal. For example, it is fundamental to good management to generate a financial return but the Return on Investment (ROI) is a check on viability. It is common in many corporations for proposals to come to the board together with an evaluation of the expected return on investment. The ROI must exceed the hurdle set by the corporation to be considered and the proposals may be ranked by ROI to allow the board to select which to approve. Without a robust strategy based on a statement of purpose, it is possible for board meeting to descend into an investor forum feeding corporate resources to where they will generate greatest financial return. Again, this leads into the trap of thinking of the corporation as a moneymaking machine.

The purpose of the corporation needs to be set as the foundation stone on which strategy is built and decisions made.

SUMMARY

- Responsibility to shareholders and other stakeholders is a fundamental non-negotiable foundation to strategic analysis.
- The statement of purpose should encapsulate a vision that can be shared by everyone close to the business to ensure that all staff pull in the same direction, investors understand what they have invested in and customers know the nature of the club they join when they buy the product or service.
- It is useful to consider the statement of purpose right at the start of the strategic process but it should be open to negotiation until the strategy is finalized.
- Teasing out the purpose of the corporation is not about defining where it is now, but where it is going. Four questions about the purpose of the corporation are useful in setting strategic direction:

1. Is this something that is *needed*?
2. Is this something *special*?
3. Is this something that is *enduring*?
4. Is this something *wanted*?

PART II

STRATEGIC APPRAISAL

Strategic appraisal is the examination of issues which may have fundamental significance to wring out a series of deductions required to craft resilient strategy. Sound strategy endures, providing the framework, whilst a storm of short-term challenges rock the corporation. The steadfastness of purpose provided by a good strategic appraisal allows strategies to emerge that can transform the corporation, guide corporate planning and provide the context for taking major decisions, particularly with regard to investment.

Looking at the world through the blinkers of business-as-usual is the normal day-to-day life of an executive or senior manager, but without making the space for deeper thinking a business can become stuck in a rut and vulnerable. The viewpoint of external consultants is often little better as they deliver analysis that will get their invoice paid, rather than take the risk of challenging the status quo. Students and practitioners of strategy will be familiar with the evolution of 'new' strategic concepts that pop up from the management literature to become the flavour of the moment for consultants and strategy experts. Being in the know about the latest buzz words is to show how well-informed you are about the latest management thinking. There is a whole language that MBA graduates are proud to display and those who don't know it are soon exposed. This would be an amusing game if it were not that the consequences can be strategies that have little bearing on the real world.

Visionary thinking is required, based on clear-eyed pragmatism and objective analysis of a hugely complex world. The potential complexity can be mind-numbing, requiring structured analysis that can identify the key drivers and tease out the issues that will have most impact. There is no single way to carry out a strategic appraisal – in the same way that there is no perfect strategy – but there is a logical sequence that can be followed to bring order to what can otherwise be a difficult task. In a changing world, corporations need to be nimble and able to adapt to altered circumstances in order to survive and thrive – or be left behind.

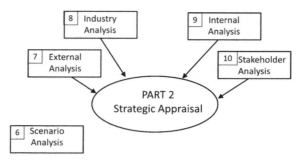

Figure P2.1   Structure Part II

In the next five chapters, a methodology is outlined designed to provide a sufficient and effective strategic appraisal. Chapter 6 opens out the analysis to the wide range of issues surrounding the corporation and encapsulates the findings in scenarios of the future. These park some of the uncertainties inherent in strategic analysis to be used later when strategic options are considered. In Chapters 7–10 more focussed analysis is provided to examine external influences, industry factors, internal issues and stakeholder matters, building up a series of insights to complete the strategic appraisal.

CHAPTER 6

SCENARIO ANALYSIS

Scenario analysis is a way to separate that which can be controlled from that which is outside the corporation's control.

At the start of the strategic process all options are open and all assumptions should be challenged. This is no time for foggy thinking or going with the flow of industry expectations. Thinking 'outside the box' is required because strategic appraisal is full of dilemmas without simple solutions. Setting strategy has as much certainty as a game of poker where you need to know the logic of the situation but be willing to think laterally and entertain counterintuitive ideas as well as expect the unexpected through observing clues (with greater clarity than those around you) which may not even be part of the central game. The strategist should open the aperture of the analysis to the full complexity of the surrounding world employing clear logic and ensuring that the analysis is objective. The unexpected events that derail corporate strategy are often seen in hindsight as blindingly obvious possibilities; why are they not picked up earlier?

To be effective, strategic analysis needs to include a broad view across society and the economy – as it affects the corporation. A wide-angled lens is required but it needs to be in sharp focus. The detail and depth required can be overwhelming; the challenge is to extract relevant and precise information out of complexity and uncertainty. A tool to help bring order to the potential chaos is scenario analysis. This can extract some of the what-if thinking out to a separate process. The subsequent stages of the strategic analysis focus on that which can be controlled and should come inside the strategy. The scenario analysis looks at that which cannot be controlled but should be understood.

This chapter is presented around a simple practical framework. For those new to the idea of scenarios this may seem daunting and difficult but with experience it becomes an enjoyable and liberating process. The process is presented here using the following six steps:

1. Open the aperture
2. Zoom in
3. Choose the points of focus
4. Push out the limits
5. Construct the Scenario matrix
6. Complete the Scenarios

THE PURPOSE OF SCENARIOS

Scenarios have a variety of uses within the corporation to help departments to design products and services and plan aspects of the business. Here the focus is on the role that scenarios can play in the formulation of business strategy. Their usefulness comes late in the strategy process to test the validity of strategic options (see Figure I.1). It may be tempting to construct utopian scenarios, of the world as we believe it should be, but this could become a distraction unless clearly labelled and used with care. A degree of exaggeration can be useful but improbable or impossible assumptions should be avoided. The scenario generation is carried out in a separate or parallel process to strategy formulation. Although it is argued in this book that strategy aimed at building a better world is both right and leads to long-term commercial success, the future is not under the control of corporate aspirations so scenarios need to encompass the actualities of the real world.

1. Open the Aperture

The first stage needs a group of people with a variety of viewpoints and range of expertise from inside and outside the corporation. This group should be convened away from the day-to-day management pressures with the time and space to think and discuss freely. The selection of the members of the group is crucial to the quality of the output. There will be experts from within the corporation (not necessarily only at a senior level) and outside experts which may include people from NGOs with an interest in the corporation's line of business. These could be organization that have been critical in the past or could be critical in the future. Bringing such viewpoints inside the process (and listening to what they have to say) can bring valuable insights and reduce the risk that the corporation's actions are misunderstood.

The aim of this first stage is to list the factors and issues that could be significant to the business as it navigates into the future. This identification of potential factors and issues should be carried out without judgement or suppression of ideas. There are no limits; anything and everything should be considered including the external environment, the industry and society, as well as factors internal to the corporation although the process is primarily looking out rather than in. The result should be an unfiltered list of factors and issues in no particular order.

2. Zoom in

From the long list of issues, a short list needs to be selected. This can involve considerable discussion as the group of 'experts' discuss which issues are particularly important and why. Disagreement is useful to draw out the reasons why each issue may be important. The desired result is a list of four to six issues, in no particular order, which it is agreed are the most significant and likely to have the greatest impact. If reaching agreement proves to be difficult, the short-list may need to be longer to close the consensus.

3. Choose the Points of Focus

The short list of key issues needs to be pared down further by selecting the three issues of most significance ranked in order of importance. This is likely to initiate another debate, perhaps going over and testing some of the arguments again. The discussion will be more useful if it is focussed on the reasons why an issue might be important rather than arguing against the inclusion of an issue. However, like the deliberations in the jury room, there should be no constraints on the arguments employed. The aim is to arrive at a list of the three prime issues ranked in order.

4. Push out the Limits

The next stage is to take the issues ranked first and second and push them out to the extremes of possibility. For example, if the 'state of the economy' has been selected as a key issue, the two extremes could be 'booming' and 'crashing'. Reality is likely to be somewhere in-between but for the sake of the exercise the two extremes should be at the limits of what could occur. From experience, this stage can be particularly difficult as some issues defy logical analysis of the extreme possibilities, but through debate it should be feasible to construct diametrically opposite limits of possibility.

5. Construct the Scenario Matrix

The extreme limits of the two prime issues can be used as the axes for the scenario matrix. The example in Figure 6.1 is the scenario matrix as it might look for an analysis carried out for an off-shore wind corporation where the two prime drivers identified are the state of the 'economy' and public attitudes to 'climate change'.

This matrix has no greater significance than a convenient tool to help construct scenarios. The four quadrants represent four different scenarios of the future. These need to be named in a way that is distinctive, memorable and captures

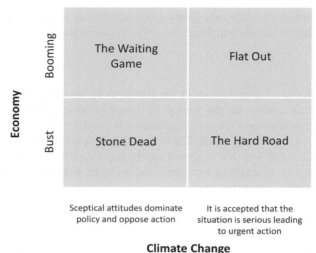

Figure 6.1   Scenario example – Off-shore wind engineering company

the essence of the future portrayed. For example, Shell, the oil corporation uses scenarios and a recent set included the scenarios 'Blueprint' and 'Scramble' (Shell 2008).[1] The former portrays a future in which there is an orderly exit from the fossil fuel economy; the latter a future where countries and corporations scramble to find a way ahead as supplies run low. These titles capture the snapshot of the future which can be used as a short-hand in later analysis. Titles which imply value judgements, such as 'good' or 'bad' should be avoided as the scenarios are outside the corporation's control and such terms imply that the corporation should be working towards one or the other. The corporation may prefer one over another but wishful thinking could take the corporation into a strategy cul-de-sac.

6. Complete the Scenarios

The scenario matrix portrays four possible scenarios but not all are needed. It is suggested here that two (or three) distinctly different scenarios will suffice. This will usually mean selecting scenarios on opposite sides of a diagonal. The next task is to flesh out the selected scenarios starting with returning to the short list of key issues. For each issue, work out how the issue is likely to play out in the scenario. If there is time, the issues on the long list can also be considered to add yet more detail. The result is descriptions of two (or three) snap shots of distinctly different possible futures.

---

1   Shell released a new set of scenarios in March 2013 named 'Mountains' and 'Oceans' showing their updated vision of plausible futures (Shell 2013).

CONCLUSION

The process described here draws together collective wisdom to bring a degree of order to complexity and generate foresight of the future. Practitioners may vary the detail of the process but retain the underlying principles of open, impartial, objective analysis of the issues most likely to impact the corporation. The scenarios are not predictions and are not to be used directly to craft strategy. They come in later to assess the validity of strategic options (over which the corporation has control) by testing how a particular strategy will perform under a variety of situations (outside the corporation's control).

The process of constructing the scenarios initiates a rich loosely structured debate leading to snapshots of the future. It can be a powerful tool if done well but can also give dangerously deluded results if regarded as an accurate portrayal of the future. The process of scenario generation should be kept separate to the other aspects of the strategic process (although of course it is useful to have members of the strategy team involved). This separation avoids wishful thinking or belief that it is possible to control factors outside the corporation's control. Scenarios are not changed to fit conveniently the strategy as it emerges but held firm as reference points frozen until there is another deep re-evaluation to generate new scenarios.

SUMMARY

- Scenario analysis provides a broad view across society and the economy identifying the key drivers without getting bogged down by complexity.
- The scenario process needs to be kept separate from the strategic analysis so that one does not confuse the other.
- The results of the scenario analysis are used later in the process of crafting strategy to test strategic options against how they fare in alternative possible futures.

CHAPTER 7

EXTERNAL ANALYSIS

Corporations with strategies which can handle disruptive change will be in the strongest position.

Scenario analysis has allowed a free format examination of the issues; this next stage is the external analysis looking for specific logical deductions to feed into the strategy formulation. Some of the uncertainty may have been parked in the scenario analysis but it would be quite wrong to allow assumptions about the continuation of business-as-usual to take hold as the analysis becomes more focussed. The aim is to identify changes about which there can be a reasonable degree of certainty. The temptation to assume that the macroeconomic context could evolve steadily, to encompass solutions to the challenges the world faces, should be avoided. Even if such a pathway for the economy can be found (politicians will try) the corporations with strategies which can handle disruptive change will be in the strongest position. Corporations that rely on business-as-usual may do well in the short-term but this could leave the corporation exposed and is not a tenable long-term strategy. It is inevitable that the current period of conflicted policy will eventually unwind as reality takes a grip of the economy and the political process; it is only the timing that is in doubt.

A key ability that the strategist should master is to understand the connectedness of the economy and society as parts of a greater whole. The interdependencies are so strong and issues so intertwined that isolated solutions, to any of the challenges the world faces, simply do not exist. Climate change cannot be tackled without a solution for energy supply; energy supply cannot be solved without changing manufacturing processes; a new paradigm of manufacturing requires the reconfiguration of supply chains; and sustainable supply chains require changes to trade policy. This is just one example of the complex daisy chains of action required. This means that when change comes, it changes everything.

This chapter will use the well-known and often used PESTEL analysis. It is exceedingly easy to fill pages with words under the required headings – as I have read in numerous MBA exam scripts over the years – but a useful analysis requires deep strategic thought and reflection. This is where I will try to steer the reader to go beyond the obvious and superficial insights to open up the analysis to a world of opportunity.

PESTEL

The core elements of the analysis are: 'Political', 'Economic', 'Social' and 'Technology'. To these core elements are added 'Environment' and 'Legal' to make the PESTEL. The potential issues to examine could fill five volumes and still only scratch the surface so this discussion focusses on the approach. The detail will depend on the corporation, its industrial sector and the countries within which it operates.

POLITICAL

The political context is important because governments set the rules of the game through policies designed to encourage what the government sees as beneficial to society and discourage activities which cause harm, supported by legislation and the rule of law. It is important that the strategic analysis identifies the relevant government policies and draws out the implications.

The most effective approach is to get inside the mind of government to understand what the government is trying to achieve. This shifts the analysis forward from the current policy debate to provide insight into the legislation in the pipeline. A step yet further is to work out what the government should be doing – even if the government does not yet know it.

Approaching the analysis from the perspective of government allows clear foresight of future policy and advanced insight that no amount of political intelligence could buy. Such deep insight can only come from analysis beyond the boundaries of the corporation's direct interest. This is another example of the benefits of using a wide-angle analytic lens. This approach is not just responsible behaviour but leads to more robust strategy.

Political appraisal by business will often lead onto political lobbying to defend the business of the corporation. This can generate a negative reaction from NGOs and sections of the press. The enlightened strategic analysis proposed here leads the corporation to understand where resistance is pointless and shifts the corporation into a space where it can lobby for those elements of future government policy that fit both a better future and the corporation's strategic direction. The latter has not been set, in the first iteration of the strategic analysis, but as the strategy takes shape the external analysis can be reviewed and further refined.

The output from the examination of the political landscape may include:

- An assessment of relevant current government policy priorities;
- An analysis of the direction of future policy; and
- Identification of areas where there is likely to be government policy when it wakes up to the issue.

ECONOMIC

The state of the economy is fundamental to the health of the business environment. A booming economy provides ample opportunity for high-margin sales whilst an economy deep in recession suffers from oversupply and tough competition. Such a simple overview is of limited use in understanding the dynamics of the real economy which is far more complex than the headline figures reported in the media.

Strategic economic analysis is difficult because of the changing economic priorities outlined in Chapter 4. The old 'certainties' of free-trade and open markets and that governments will put economic growth at the top of the policy agenda are being questioned. This may lead to a schizophrenic analysis with real economic parameters vying with delusional aspirations. It is worth including some of the more novel alternative economic policies in the analysis in case this opens up new opportunities to be exploited – if government can be persuaded to adopt them. The converse applies in that examination of existing economic policies may show flaws that indicate threats to avoid. For example, it is odd that the problems in the Eurozone came as a surprise to many politicians. The problems were logical consequences that could be predicted through an analysis of monetary union without political union. There is no need for corporations to use the political 'blind eye' but to work with the underlying logic of the situation.

Access to resources is a key part of the economic analysis. As the world economy reaches resource limits, it would be a dangerous assumption that world markets for resources will remain open. Politicians will step in to secure supplies in any way they can. Corporations should also be planning how to operate in a resource-constrained world and work through the strategic implications.

A key issue at the time of writing is the economic parameters of the transition to the low-carbon economy. This is full of opportunities and fraught with dangerous misconceptions. Making the wrong analysis here may draw deductions that go forward into the adoption of a strategic option based on a false premise (the strategic cycle should catch such errors in the next iteration of strategy but valuable time could be lost and investment misdirected before the mistake is uncovered). The global carbon market is the most glaring example of economic policy being used which is unlikely to survive as the intellectual basis is tested in the real economy (Box 7.1). If the analysis presented here is correct, the businesses that invest in the global carbon market will suffer losses as the value of carbon credits is debased.

BOX 7.1 GLOBAL CARBON MARKET

The concept of a global market for carbon dioxide emissions was included in the Kyoto Protocol[11] in an attempt to hold emissions in check. Without an alternative plan, this has survived and remains the basis of climate policy. A deep analysis of the longer-term consequences of such a market indicates that it would be unlikely to solve fossil-fuel dependency but may instead reinforce reliance on fossil fuel and slow the transition to other sources (McManners 2010). There remains considerable hope amongst climate change policy makers that a functioning global carbon market is possible so it may be some time before the flaws are exposed.

The implication for corporations is that relying on a price for carbon within a global market to support long-term investment decisions is risky. The safer strategy is to channel investment directly to reducing reliance on fossil fuel without channelling investment offshore to the vagaries of the carbon market. There is a potential role for national carbon markets but even here carbon taxes are likely to be much more predictable and effective in delivering the outcome of a low-carbon economy.

---

1   The Kyoto Protocol was adopted at the third Conference of the Parties to the UNFCCC (COP 3) in Kyoto, Japan, on 11 December 1997.

The output from the examination of the economic landscape could be highly diverse depending on the corporation, its industry and its circumstances but might include:

• An assessment of the economic conditions in key markets;
• A forecast of the availability of and access to key resources; and
• An insight into likely changes to economic policy.

SOCIAL

Social trends can have major implications for strategy. It is not just the obvious factors such as changing consumer preferences but also workforce factors and investor attitudes.

For corporations that sell products or services to consumers, understanding changing customer expectations, needs and desires is vital. However, a strategic analysis is not the same as a marketing analysis. Marketing departments have become adept at building brands and influencing people through advertizing to persuade them that they need the corporation's products and planting the idea that people 'must' have the latest model or newest version. Strategic analysis should steer clear of the marketing hype and remain down-to-earth. Questions to ask are:

- Which of the corporation's products or services are needed by customers?
- Which of the corporation's products or services are desired by customers?
- Which of the corporation's products or services sell because people are persuaded through advertizing that they are desirable?

In the first category are essential products or services and the basis of a sustainable line of business. In the second category, these are discretionary expenditure where revenue is less dependable. The third category is of uncertain real value and could suffer badly if there is a backlash against vacuous consumerism. Strategy should focus on real needs and desires. This is not only responsible but is a good test of which business units are only kept afloat by marketing spend – a precarious situation if allowed to continue.

Society is the market place and the pool from which the corporation draws its workforce. Change in people's attitudes and expectations can influence the competition to recruit talent. An example is the growing trend for bright young graduates to want to work for corporations which share their aspirations for a better world. There is also the cost of labour to factor into strategic analysis to influence decisions about where to locate production; it should be remembered that this is not a simple arithmetic calculation based on costs alone. The workforce can also be part of the corporation's network influencing other consumers and government. The strategic analysis should look beyond the narrow economic case (cheap labour and/or maximized automation) to examine the strategic value of an engaged and content workforce established within the markets in which the corporation operates. Such value is easily overlooked using simple accountancy measures.

Ethical investing is a growing trend to consider and could be used to the corporation's advantage. There have always been individual investors with ethical and altruistic motives but the concept of 'ethical investing' applying to investment funds and pension schemes is relatively new. The market is not yet convinced that these can provide strong returns (Insley 2013). However, fund managers answer to customers, and customers are starting to require ethical conduct. This is not simply a matter of wanting their funds to be put to ethical use but, more importantly, to reduce risk in a world where unethical behaviour can have severe commercial consequences. A prime example is *Nike* which suffered badly in the 1990s when the working conditions in its factories in South East Asia were exposed (Ballinger 1992) leading to a massive consumer boycott which forced the corporation to change its culture (Birch 2012).

The output from the examination of social issues and social trends can have deep strategic significance, not only for how and where the corporation sells but how and where to recruit as well as influence how to structure and organize production.

TECHNOLOGY

Technology is important for corporate strategy in the current era of 'open innovation' and will remain important as 'responsible innovation' takes over. For some corporations, technology is at the heart of the business and innovation is the lifeblood that keeps it running. For others, technology is an operational necessity but in all cases technology matters and its strategic importance is hard to overemphasize.

Technology can be a great enabler of corporate strategy, when based on disruptive technologies developed in the corporation's research facilities and protected by patent. Technology can also be a great destroyer, as old technologies – and possibly whole industries – become obsolete in successive waves of Schumpeterian creative destruction.

The timescale of technology renewals is shortening. This is partly due to the effort expended by governments and corporations working with academia to drive forward innovation, establishing clusters of expertise, thus reducing the time required to go from research laboratory to market. Instead of waiting for the next disruptive technology to arrive, there is huge pressure to deploy new technologies quickly before the full consequences have been fully tested.

The management and control of technical innovation will evolve as government and responsible business exert tighter control, taking technology deployment beyond the era of innovation into the era of responsibility. In the innovation era, new technologies have been deployed in pursuit of the commercial opportunities with little regard, initially, for the social and environmental consequences. These are picked up by government post implementation leading to regulations and controls following evidence of the damage. This is inefficient and irresponsible.

The responsible deployment of technology will be in support of problems that need a solution and any new technology assessed with some of the same rigour so far reserved for drugs for human use. There can be a marked strategic difference between leveraging commercial advantage from a technology and using technology to deliver the solution to a problem. For example, the technology of LED lighting offers a step-change in lighting efficiency. Marketing day-light intensity indoor lighting solutions to sell more LED lights (for the same levels of energy consumption) is a possible commercial approach. The responsible deployment of this technology is to reduce energy consumption as part of closing the gap between demand for energy and the realistic aspirations for renewable energy supply. This is what government will want to achieve and business should act to be part of the solution rather than simply maximize short-term sales.

The replacement of old technology with new patented technology, and marketing it as 'new and cool', is deeply engrained business practice. Society needs a more responsible approach – although there is little sign that this will happen any time soon. Over the coming decades ways will be found to bring technological developments under tighter control. Corporations would be wise to become familiar with taking a responsible approach in advance of legislation and controls.

The output from the examination of technological issues will be different for each corporation. The strategic analysis of technology as it affects the bigger picture should examine both areas of growth and areas where decline might be expected. Universal technologies are of particular interest, which change the nature of business – as we have seen with the impact of the internet over the first decade of this century. This short section provides an insight into the new mindset that will shape the next phase of technical progress which is describe here as 'responsible innovation'.

The output from the examination of technology issues could include:

- A register of the corporation's key technologies and capabilities, particularly those backed up by patent;
- Emerging technologies and trends that could reconfigure the industry; and
- Technologies with the potential to transform society or the economy.

ENVIRONMENT

The environment is a fundamental constraint on society, the economy and business. Every corporation draws resources from the environment, operates facilities residing in the environment and sells to customers who live in the environment. The ecosystem and ecosystem services are not merely an external constraint but an integral part of the wider systems of human activity on a finite planet.

A dispassionate logical analysis can be difficult in a polarized debate, with some environmentalists blocking everything without discriminating good projects from flawed projects (Box 7.2) and some corporations believing that the environment is none of their business except in so far as they comply with regulations.

BOX 7.2 IRRATIONAL ENVIRONMENTALISM – BRENT SPAR

In 1995 Shell proposed sinking an obsolete oil production platform, the Brent Spar in the North Sea. There was a furore orchestrated by Green Peace including a boycott of the company's retail outlets. The company caved in to the pressure and changed the plan to dismantle the platform on land at much greater expense. Subsequent analysis showed that the corporation's original plan was the best environmental option (Fisheries Research Services 2004) – as Green Peace later admitted. The respected journal *Nature* described Shell Oil's decision not to sink the used oil-rig at sea as a 'needless dereliction of rationality' going on to say that 'The irony in this episode, which … has done no credit to Shell … is that the environmental effect on deep-sea life of dumping the Brent Spar would be minimal or even beneficial.' (*Nature* 1995)

How could Shell have mounted a better defence of its actions?

To counter irrational environmentalism corporations should develop deep understanding of how they interact with the environment and engage in an open and transparent debate to earn the trust of society as they seek permission to operate. Ambivalence is dangerous. Total commitment to excellent environmental stewardship is the best defence against irrational environmentalism.

The strategic analysis of environmental issues should take place with the same clear objective view as for the other PESTEL factors. The passionate environmental debate is now focussed on climate change. This is at least a clear-cut issue: the science is clear, burning fossil fuel is changing the climate and the consequences, although hard to predict accurately, could be severe. Policy makers must start closing down the fossil fuel economy without further delay. This plain fact should be a building block of all resilient corporate strategies from now forward but there are more serious environmental challenges beyond climate change.

The most serious environmental risk is biodiversity loss, which is a huge risk to the stability of the ecosystem and its ability to adjust and adapt. The loss of natural habitats and deforestation are time bombs ticking away which will require a strategic response. Any corporation complicit in such activities will suffer as governments take action and society turns against further destruction of the world's natural capital. There is a huge wave of policy and regulation which could arise when this danger is accepted and understood (McManners 2008, 2009 and 2010) but it is beyond the scope of this book.

Assessing and quantifying the corporation's environmental impact is the foundation of the strategic environmental analysis. Following this, the analysis should look for opportunities to reduce the negative impacts. The most interest stage of the analysis – a new approach in corporate strategy – is to consider how corporate activities could be reconfigured to engage with defending and rebuilding ecosystem services. Corporate environmentalism based on end-of-pipe pollution control will be replaced with ecosystem-compatible manufacturing processes and total life-cycle design. Corporations that have not yet begun thinking through the consequences are already behind the curve. Actual progress to date has been slow but the concepts are well understood and the implementation is feasible. Government legislation is slow in coming but we can be sure that the legislative steamroller will gather pace. Corporate strategy should plan to be well ahead of legislation, with firm plans in place, but implementation timed carefully so the corporation is not exposed to significantly higher costs, making products uncompetitive, leading into the transition.

The output from the examination of environmental issues may include:

• A register of major environmental impacts;
• An assessment of current and pending relevant environmental legislation;
• Identification of opportunities to improve environmental performance, particularly relative to competitors;
• Where the corporation sells products, an assessment of the feasibility and consequences of shifting to total life-cycle manufacturing processes;
• A report on how the corporation could reconfigure activities to defend and rebuild ecosystem (perhaps through linking up with an academic or NGO organisation), remaining open to novel solutions but including a robust test of commercial viability.

LEGAL

Responsible corporations should, of course, operate within the law in all the countries in which they operate. This is a fact of doing business so usually regarded as an operational constraint rather than of strategic interest. However, changes in legislation should be monitored as the period of introduction of new laws could have strategic implications.

The aspects of the law that have strategic importance will vary from corporation to corporation. There is little point trying to cover these here but there is a general decision to be taken with regard to legal compliance. It is important to decide within the strategy process whether to have a policy of compliance with the letter of the law or with the spirit of the law. In my own career I have always chosen to comply with the spirit of the law and have enjoyed reduced costs for legal and financial services – as well as sleeping easy at night – but this not a common approach.

A common approach in business is to only comply with the letter of the law – which is a perfectly legal choice. The policies of de-regulation and measuring success by shareholder value have tended to encourage compliance with the letter of the law to be able to maximize the apparent financial gain. A recent example is a number of MNCs operating in Britain have used loopholes in the accounting rules to avoid paying corporation tax, in some cases paying no tax at all, in the UK despite reporting strong profits to shareholders from UK operations (Bergin 2012). This has saved the corporations millions of pounds but as the press, NGOs and activists found out what was happening the backlash in consumer boycotts and bad publicity has impacted the corporations involved. At a personal level, senior executives were summoned to appear before The Parliamentary Select Committee where they received a hostile grilling (House of Commons 2012). Interestingly, some commentators reported that the impact of the bad publicity is short lived (Barford and Holt 2013) and less costly than the amounts saved through the tax avoidance implying executives should accept their dressing down and carry on regardless. Such a narrow perspective could encourage management to continue on their current path despite antagonizing government (House of Lords 2013) and increasing the risk of legislation which could have significant long-term cost implications.

The strategic analysis requires a balanced assessment between 'compliance with the letter of the law' or a policy of 'compliance with the spirit of the law'. The former is likely to maximize direct financial gain but has associated risks. The latter accepts that short-term financial gain may be compromised but risks are less and legal costs avoided. This direction has to come from the top and is a strategic matter because there is no point having different policies in different divisions because wherever dubious business practice is exposed, it will reflect on the whole corporation. The strategy should be to either comply with the letter of the law or the spirit of the law but avoid getting stuck in the middle.

If the trend of the last two decades could be reversed and corporate policy shifted towards compliance with the spirit and intention of the law, it might persuade government to slash red-tape and reduce the complexity of regulations to give responsible corporations, increased freedom to operate.

The output from the examination of legal issues could include:

- Impending changes in the law with strategic significance;
- An assessment of the corporation's current approach to legal compliance and how this meshes with current trends in society;
- A recommendation for the principle of legal compliance to be deployed in the future and how this might change the relations the corporation has with government and other agencies.

CONCLUSION

The output from the PESTEL analysis is a collection of observations, issues and factors arising from the analysis of the macro external environment. It becomes easier to draw upon this analysis if these can be ordered in some way. Looking for the relationship between factors, deductions and deeper insights is the way forward. A number of factors may coalesce into themes and link into logical chains. An obvious example is: concern over climate change caused by emissions from fossil fuel; connects with economic consequences of high fuel costs; connects with the potential of low-carbon technologies; and comes together in a persuasive case to channel corporate resources into solutions that replace fossil-fuel dependency. It will not always be so obvious and the most valuable insights may take considerable effort to tease out through reflecting at the end of the PESTEL analysis on what should be carried forward in the analysis.

SUMMARY

The output from the external analysis is a collection of insights, issues and factors to be drawn upon in crafting possible strategic options:

- *Political* factors may include an assessment of relevant government policy priorities and the direction of future policy;
- *Economic* factors may include an assessment of the economic conditions in key markets, availability of key resources and an insight into likely changes to economic policy;
- *Social* issues identified may include trends and attitudes affecting sales, recruitment and even influence how to structure and organize production;
- *Technology* factors will vary highly between industries and may include a general shift from the current era of 'open innovation' to 'responsible innovation';
- *Environmental* issues may include an assessment of current and pending relevant environmental legislation and identification of opportunities to improve environmental performance relative to competitors;
- *Legal* issues may include impending changes in the law with strategic significance and an assessment of the corporation's current approach to legal compliance.

CHAPTER 8

INDUSTRY ANALYSIS

The 6-Forces model introduced here is a new model for a new era.

Each industry has its own dynamics depending on the range of commercial players, the nature of the activities and the historic path the industry has followed to reach the point at which the analysis is carried out. The aim of this stage of the strategic analysis is to understand the workings of the industry, identifying points of strength, points of weakness and fault lines that can be exploited.

In this chapter, a generic model is outlined which can be applied to any industry. Each particular analysis will flow according to what is discovered but these general parameters provide a sufficient framework.

INDUSTRY ECOSYSTEM

Industries operate like ecosystems with a dynamic balance between corporations, each of which fills a particular niche. The school of competitive strategy looks at the industry ecosystem from a Darwinian perspective where the fittest survive. It is now understood that competition is only one aspect of ecosystem theory with cooperation amongst species much more important than simple Darwinism would imply (Rubenstein and Kealey 2012). The same is true for industry ecosystems (Smith et al. 1995) which by their nature are highly competitive but the cooperation between players is also a powerful force. Alliances can have huge strategic significance which is not reflected fully in the simple theory of competitive strategy. Examples are the Oneworld alliance amongst airlines established in 1999 and the alliance between Disney and HP which has been running since 1938 when Disney purchased eight oscillators from HP founders Bill Hewlett and Dave Packard for use in the sound design of *Fantasia*.

Industry dynamics can be modelled as a balance between competing and cooperating forces. Focussing only on competition leads into a zero-sum game of ever leaner corporations as each corporation fights for the leadership position. The need to fight can be reduced if competition is balanced with cooperation.

Understanding this balance leads to more effective strategy. A couple of analogies reinforce the point. First, for sports teams, good players are useful but they don't need to be the best players in the league if the team is strong. On the other hand a team with the best players and weak team work will surely fail. A corporation does not need to be the best, but can be on par with the best, provided it is teamed up with corporations also operating on a par with the best, so that together they make a winning combination. The second example is military commanders fighting a war. This is an environment of severe competition where at the tactical level it is a matter of life and death. Even so, at the strategic level, it is important to look beyond winning battles to build the alliances that will lead to a successful outcome.

Each industry ecosystem nestles within the greater ecosystem of the economy as a dynamic balance between competing and cooperating players. Understanding this balance for a particular industry should be one of the foundation stones of strategic appraisal.

6-FORCES MODEL

The 6-Forces model introduced here is a new model for a new era. It replaces Michael Porter's 5-Forces model (Porter 1979) which has been the staple of the micro analysis of an industry since the 1980s. Porter's starting assumption was that industries are shaped by competitive forces. The new model presented here is based on the assumption that industries are shaped by a balance between competition and cooperation. To avoid adding yet more terminology to the lexicon

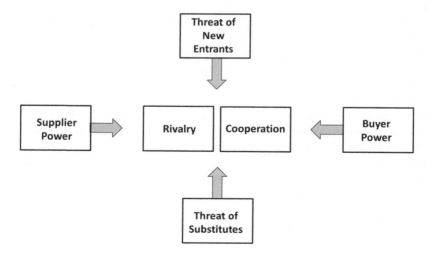

Figure 8.1   6-Forces model

of strategy, the terminology introduced by Porter is retained adding the force: 'cooperation amongst industry players'. It should be noted that despite retaining Porter's terminology the 6-Forces model is not 5-Forces +1; but arises from different starting assumptions and requires a different mind-set to apply the model effectively.

RIVALRY

At the tactical level, business is all about rivalry, winning bids and competing for customers. Rivalry is good for an industry keeping players strong and efficient – provided success comes from winning business on merit. Rivalry focussed on extinguishing competitors is a destructive process likely to lead only to short-term advantage. For example, starting a price war, selling goods or services at or below cost, can seem like a reasonable tactic from a competitive viewpoint if you are confident your corporation has the deepest pockets to be left standing whilst competitors go out of business. From a balanced strategic viewpoint this looks like desperation; it would be better to compete on excelling in some way leaving space for your competitors to do the same. They might respond with creating their own special niche whilst you dominate the niche you have carved out. Of course the competitor might not be up to the challenge and go out of business as part of the natural process of dynamic change but responsible corporations understand that the focus has to be on improving products and services not on executing competitors.

Intense rivalry makes doing business harder but this can be beneficial in improving corporate performance illustrated by the sporting analogy in Box 8.1.

BOX 8.1 THE ADVANTAGES OF INTENSE RIVALRY

The state of middle distance track athletics in the UK in the 1970s and early 1980s is an interesting case study in the beneficial effects of intense rivalry. Two UK athletes dominated this era, Seb Coe and Steve Ovett. They were rivals in domestic races and team mates in international events representing Great Britain. If either of these great athletes had not had the other, then winning at UK events would have been easy. As it was, to win domestic races they faced each other, making the competition and rivalry intense. To be the best in the UK was much tougher than it would otherwise have been so that when these rivals came together to cooperate as team mates at world level they were, for a time, invincible. Over a number of years they dominated the world athletics stage including famously the 1980 Olympics in Moscow where they both came away with a gold medal. The intense rivalry made it more difficult for them, but also brought greater success to both athletes. Their focus was not on causing injury or harm to their opponent but to run faster than their team mate in pursuit of shared excellence. The rivalry made them both raise their game. This analogy shows how rivalry within an industry can be beneficial for corporations provided success comes from winning business on merit.

Intense rivalry can drive down short-term profits but it can also strengthen the industry to make it harder for new entrants and build industries that are strong within the greater economy. However, where rivalry is the much stronger force, compared with cooperation, profitability can suffer in a scramble to maintain market share.

COOPERATION

Industries are not just made up of corporations out-competing each other but there are a whole series of cooperative arrangements, formal and informal. It is easier to work alongside an ally than to fight a rival. Responsible alliance building can balance competition and preserve profitability to be able to grow an industry where all players have the chance to thrive. Where this degenerates into cartels and profiteering this is a sign of trouble to come as government is forced to step in and regulate. Healthy cooperation, balanced with healthy competition, builds a sustainable industry for all players.

NEW ENTRANTS

Industry incumbents are always under threat from potential new entrants. The industry is less at risk if there are high entry barriers such as patents and the need for large investment. Strong existing alliances within the industry are also a good defence. New entrants have to fight their way into the market finding a niche which they can fill better than the incumbents. Usually it is only after winning a foothold that the new entrant will be in a position to balance its competitive strategy with cementing its place in the structure of the industry through building alliances. There is a special case where a new entrant can come in under the radar by building alliances as its launch pad but only if it has something clearly unique and special to be embraced by the current industry networks.

An industry is attractive if there are high barriers to entry including strong industry networks that make entry difficult for new arrivals.

SUBSTITUTES

The industry as a whole is always under the threat of substitute products or services. For example in Telecoms, voice-over-internet protocol (VoIP) is a substitute for traditional phone calls. Telecoms companies that stick rigidly to phone services will be caught out. For each incumbent corporation to monitor the risks can be a heavy overhead. One approach is for industry players to come together in scanning the horizon for potential substitutes more effectively than acting alone. This might go further, through cooperative arrangements, to shift the threat to an opportunity; to in effect sow the seeds of the industry's future destruction from within. In Telecoms, VoIP is being integrated into services with mobile phones that offer both. Through strong industry networks the threat of substitutes can be neutered and used as the basis to transform the industry as each corporation focusses on securing its niche in the changing industry landscape supported by research carried out by industry organizations.

POWER OF SUPPLIERS

An industry dominated by one or two suppliers is not attractive because the suppliers can grab a large share of the value, whereas if there are many potential suppliers, their bargaining power is low. A strong position for a corporation within an industry is to ensure it has a range of reliable suppliers, encouraging competition between them but also building close cooperation with a few favoured suppliers to give them confidence to invest in improving their capability to supply the corporation. Once again, the industry is stable when competition balances with cooperation.

POWER OF BUYERS

An industry serving a few buyers is not attractive because they have the power to dictate terms. An industry is more attractive where there are many buyers so their power is low. The sign of a good defence against buyer power is to occupy a particular niche within the industry ecosystem where the corporation provides a product or service which is the customer's first choice. Instead of attempting to sell to all buyers, the incumbent corporations can target particular segments with the informal collective aim of growing the industry serving the buyers with tailored products and services. The buyers get a better product and their power to drive a bargain is reduced producing a healthy balance between cooperation and competition.

An attractive industry shows a good balance between competition and cooperation, where there are strong barriers to entry for potential new entrants, the industry networks are on the lookout for potential substitutes, suppliers are being managed affectively and buyer power has been neutered by the incumbents adopting an informal arrangement to target particular segments. An unattractive industry is where competition is the dominant force, barriers to entry are low, a few suppliers are in control and there are a limited number of buyers.

GOVERNMENT PERSPECTIVE

The 6-Forces model is presented here from an industry perspective but the model can also be used by government and other agencies wanting to improve industry performance. The model encourages government to focus on improving the balance between competition and cooperation. Where government policy is focussed on competition alone, this can be counterproductive, unless it is balanced with facilitating industry networks and cooperation. The UK rail industry is an example (Box 8.2).

BOX 8.2 UK RAIL INDUSTRY

The UK rail industry was privatized by the instrument of the Railways Act 1993. This established a model of competition without applying the principle presented in this book of ensuring a balance between competition and cooperation. This has led to an industry with fundamental inefficiencies such as a wide variety of rolling stock across the rail network as separate train operating companies fight to squeeze maximum financial return from their time-limited franchises. From a corporate perspective, the companies involved are generally making good profits but the total government subsidy going into the railways in the twenty years since privatization has roughly trebled to reach £6billion (Wellings 2013). Although there are a number of reasons for this increase, it does not look like an efficient outcome from the government's perspective. If the 6-Forces model had been applied to the UK rail industry, at the time when privatization was being considered, the government might have set up a more sustainable structure with a natural balance. Establishing a framework focussed on competition overseen by a regulator has incentivized the train operators to game the system instead of running an efficient railway, costing the government more not less. Both responsible government and responsible rail companies should welcome shifting the balance, from pure competition, to competition balanced with cooperation.

In conclusion, the industry analysis is looking for the extent to which there is an effective balance between competition and cooperation. An unbalanced industry is likely to struggle whilst a well-balanced industry is likely to be profitable and sustainable. The 6-Forces analytic framework provides a way to corral the issues and draw out the dynamics of the industry.

In summary, the output from the industry analysis is likely to include:

- An assessment of the balance between competition and cooperation;
- An evaluation of the strength of barriers to entry for new entrants;
- Whether the industry is at risk from substitutes and whether the industry is geared up to cope;
- An analysis of the suppliers and buyers;

- An overall assessment of whether this is an attractive industry including identification of fault lines or niches within the industry that need to be filled – or will need to be filled as the industry evolves.

CHAPTER 9

INTERNAL ANALYSIS

Strategy is about navigating the next stage of the corporation's journey but the starting point is where the corporation is now.

The aim of the internal strategic appraisal is to make a high-level inventory of corporate assets to provide a resource-based view to complement the external view. Strategic ideas can arise from the opportunities identified in the external analysis or build on the capabilities identified in the internal analysis. When it comes to crafting strategy, the best use should be made of both the external opportunities identified and the internal resources available within the corporation, supplemented by additional capabilities that may be required.

In this chapter, a check list is provided to support the internal analysis but it is not exhaustive. The strategist should look across the corporation with an open mind picking out anything of strategic significance.

HISTORIC PATH

The heritage of the corporation has been built up over the life of the corporation, collecting assets, developing resources – and collecting liabilities. In addition to tangible assets such as facilities, plant and equipment, the corporation will have intangible assets such as reputation, brands, know-how as well as culture and values. All of these can be changed to suit new circumstances but it is sensible to build strategy making use of existing resources (and aiming to divest assets that no longer have a strategic purpose). Strategy is about navigating the next stage of the corporate journey but there is little point in deciding that it would be better not to start from here; the corporation is where it is, and strategy should leverage the best from the situation.

STRATEGIC ASSETS

An inventory of the main strategic assets is a set of building blocks to feed into the strategic process. These may not be sufficient but making use of assets that are already owned makes sense. There are numerous types of asset including:

- Patents
- Access rights (to natural resources for example)
- Significant industrial facilities
- Site and land
- Brands

STRATEGIC LIABILITIES

An inventory of the main strategic liabilities acts as a strategic risk register. Liabilities can undermine strategy, particularly if they are hidden liabilities waiting to be exposed. It is recommended that the analysis should focus on assets with considerable value on the balance sheet; are these values real or fiction? Is the asset likely to become a stranded asset as the business landscape changes? An asset which the corporation believes has considerable value now, but which will become worthless as the new strategic direction takes shape, is of particular significance. The strategy will have to include a plan to divest such assets whilst they still have a value in the market. There are numerous types of liability including:

- Access rights for resources that may not be in demand in the future (such as coal reserves);
- Sites contaminated by the activities of the corporation;
- Long-term health problems relating to the corporation's products or services for which the corporation may be liable;
- Pension liabilities (if the scale is of strategic significance).

STRATEGIC CAPABILITIES

In addition to tangible and intangible strategic assets and liabilities the corporation may have certain capabilities at which it excels and does better than other corporations. These may be specific expertise, or bundles of expertise, which provide a special capability. These could be, for example, supply-chain expertise, advanced engineering excellence or a powerful research capability. It is not possible here to provide a comprehensive list; the analysis should trawl through the corporation identifying and picking out the key aspects. It may not be obvious where potential value lies if it is not currently fully exploited. It may require lateral thinking to connect dormant capabilities with the possibility of leveraging them within the new corporate strategy.

OTHER CORPORATE FEATURES

The McKinsey 7S framework is useful as a further level of internal analysis. The 7S include the hard elements of structure, strategy, and systems with the soft elements of, skills, style (of leadership) and staff. Shared values are the culture and core values of the corporation.

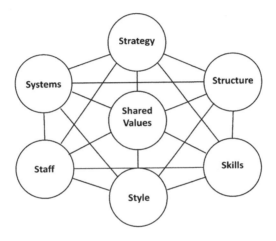

Figure 9.1   McKinsey 7S framework

Each of the seven internal aspects of the organization should be considered looking for insights with strategic significance. In particular, consideration should be given to how the elements interrelate. An effective corporation should have the elements aligned and this balance needs to be maintained. The depth of the analysis depends on the circumstances discovered and the perceived need for realignment.

SUMMARY

This short chapter on internal analysis is an introduction to what might be a deep and full analysis depending on the situation encountered. The result could be a number of insights which might, but does not have to, include:

• Register of main strategic assets;

- Register of main strategic liabilities;
- The identification of strategic capabilities, with possible ways they could be leveraged;
- A selected list of internal issues with strategic significance.

CHAPTER 10

STAKEHOLDER ANALYSIS

The corporation is obligated to its stakeholders.

The aim of stakeholder analysis is to gather information on the entities with interest in, or influence over, the strategic direction of the corporation. The needs and opinions of shareholders are clearly important, as are the views of the community of people directly under the umbrella of the corporation such as employees. The extent to which strategy takes account of other stakeholders is a matter of judgement.

In this chapter, the focus is on gathering sufficient stakeholder information to inform the strategic analysis. This should include the key requirements of the most significant stakeholders. There are many other stakeholder groups than those discussed here that could be of interest depending on the corporation and the nature of its business.

POWER/INTEREST

To focus the analysis where it can be most useful, the potentially important stakeholders should be plotted on the Power/Interest matrix shown in Figure 10.1 (overleaf).

Stakeholders in Quadrant 1 have considerable interest in the corporation's strategy and considerable power; clearly their interests should be taken into account. Quadrants 2 and 3 should be considered and the depth of analysis will depend on what is discovered. For Quadrant 4, stakeholders with little interest and little power might be worth a glance to check that there are not exceptional circumstances but generally it is not worth expending time and resources on the stakeholders in this quadrant.

The process of analysis should include consulting stakeholders but it could also involve analysing their needs in an exercise which does not include them. The reason for this is that strategic analysis should take into account stakeholder concerns but, in the final analysis, the best strategy should be selected. Almost

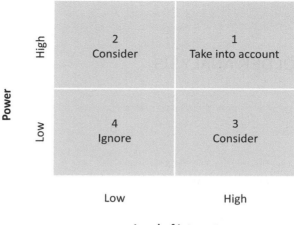

Figure 10.1   Power/Interest matrix

certainly there will some stakeholders who oppose the most appropriate strategic direction and they should not be allowed to hold the strategic process to ransom. A degree of confidentiality and closed-door analysis may be required. This could apply to the views of employees, opinions of NGOs or even to the views of shareholders.

SHAREHOLDERS

Where individual shareholders can be identified, it is important to discover their aims and intentions.

For companies in private ownership there may be a clearly defined register of individual investors. Finding out their intentions, particularly the timescale over which they expect a return can be a valuable insight. At a later stage, it may be necessary to seek to influence who is on the shareholder register, to recruit new investors and allow other current shareholders to depart (typically those with a short time horizon such as a VC with short-term targets that may hinder building long-term value).

For listed corporations, it is useful to examine the share register for large blocks of shares held by particular investment funds so that the manager can be identified and brought inside the strategic thinking. Investors with long time horizons, and able to offer continuous long-term support, should be nurtured and retained providing some respite from the short-termism of the markets.

In some cases shareholders may have objectives other than simply a financial return. Such active investors are currently rare but in the new investment environment more shareholders can be expected to find ways to flex their muscles to look beyond the raw financial figures to the corporation's wider impact. When large investors, such as pension funds, adopt objectives that align with their member's wider interests they could become a powerful force in the market. It may be strategically significant to seek to attract such long-term investors.

At the end of the strategic process, it will be important to be able to 'sell' the strategy to shareholders; so including a shareholder analysis in the initial strategic appraisal can be a valuable exercise.

EMPLOYEES

The staff can be one of the corporation's most valuable assets but they are only owned to the extent that they have employment contracts. A poorly managed strategic appraisal, which sows seeds of doubt, may ease out the very people the corporation needs. The approach should be forward looking and positive with any tough choices that might affect employees kept confidential until late in the process.

Despite the need for confidentiality over the detail, there should also be employee engagement. The strategy will have to be sold to staff so bringing the staff inside the appraisal process will make this easier. Such engagement can also generate new ideas and deeper insights from staff representatives brought inside the discussion who then understand the pressures the corporation is under. Where it looks likely that the corporation will have to make tough choices, staff representatives may be the source of ideas, such as changing terms of employment to preserve jobs, which would be fiercely resisted if proposed by management working alone.

At the end of the strategic process, when decisions have been made, there should be a clear announcement about the impact on staff and jobs focussed on reassuring and strengthening the corporate community.

COMMUNITIES

The corporation could be playing a role in a number of communities such as the localities where corporate factories and facilities are sited. These can provide considerable indirect support such as workers and their accommodation as well as permission to operate. The focus of strategic analysis should be on the resources of the community and the power structures that the corporation needs to navigate to manage community relations. Sound corporate strategy will include enduring commitment to communities to foster durable support in a win-win relationship. The ideas prevalent in Corporate Social Responsibility (CSR) should not be allowed to obscure the strategic significance of communities. Of course there are reputation and public relations angles but strategic analysis should look beyond this at what both parties gain from the relationship.

Factories or facilities that are at the heart of a community should be identified and their concerns and needs brought into the strategic appraisal. It may arise that in the final analysis a facility has to be closed, but not before the community has been given ample opportunity to discuss alternatives. The joint dialogue between corporation and the host community can throw up unexpected and unanticipated ideas to increase the synergy between corporate and community objectives to mutual advantage.

GOVERNMENT

Government has, indirectly, the ultimate veto over corporate strategy. If the government does not like how a corporation is behaving, it can legislate to change the rules of the game. It is clearly important that strategy avoids fostering the ire of government in order to retain the freedom to operate. It is less obvious that to go further and get inside governmental thinking allows the corporation to steal a march on its competitors. What is the government view on the corporation's or industry's activities? How will this view change as the government faces up to the challenges of environmental degradation and threats to social cohesion? This analysis is particularly important when examining the corporation's international operations where weak governments could switch policy quickly in response to popular pressure (or strong governments operating to a nationalist or ideological agenda).

CUSTOMERS

Satisfying customers is the lifeblood of the corporation running through the operating activities from product design and marketing to sales and service. At the strategic level, it is important to look beyond the product or service to what it is that the corporation provides that customers value. The key information required is: why customers are attracted to the corporation, why do they stay and if they leave, for what reason? Strategic insight comes from looking at the customer as a stakeholder providing a different insight to viewing the customer as a punter.

Corporate strategy can go badly astray when customers are seen as a source of revenue rather than a stakeholder in the corporation. The miss-selling of payment protection insurance (PPI) by UK banks is a case in point.

PPI is a product which is sold not bought i.e. consumers rarely set out to buy this product on their own. Instead, cover is promoted in some way by the distributor of the associated credit. (OFT 2006:6)

In many cases, the sales PPI was designed to squeeze money out of customers through abusing the customer relationship to persuade people to buy something they did not seek and did not need (Box 10.1).

BOX 10.1 PAYMENT PROTECTION INSURANCE (PPI)

The UK banking sector made £-billions selling PPI alongside credit and loans through the 1990s and 2000s. Bank employees dealing with customers gave the impression of giving advice but were acting under instructions to push sales of PPI products because the premiums were a useful addition to profits. This was a classic example of treating customers as revenue streams to be milked rather than customers to be served. In many cases the insurance was of little value and in some cases the circumstances of the borrower were such that it would have been impossible to ever claim on the policy. When the scale of the miss-selling was exposed, regulators intervened with the UK Competition Commission finally bringing the practice under control in their order of 2011 (Competition Commission 2011). It is estimated that the total cost to UK banks of paying compensation is in excess of £15 billion.

Strategy based on selling to customers is likely to involve a tough competition over price; strategy that deals with customers as stakeholders can build a relationship in which price is not the ruling factor. An example is Apple where the customer is brought inside the corporation building a loyalty that overrides value for money. Devices with same functionality can be bought for much less but Apple has succeeded in selling something that transcends the product. The strategic appraisal of customers aims to draw out what it is about the corporation customers buy into (and what puts them off).

OTHER CORPORATIONS

Through the lens of competitive strategy, it seems odd to include other corporations as stakeholders but considering them as stakeholders the analysis shifts towards the more balanced strategic approach championed in this book. Corporations that are 'complementors' or 'suppliers' are stakeholders and should be treated as such. Understanding their motives can ensure strategy prevents complementors from becoming competitors and encourages suppliers to invest to improve their ability to continue to supply the corporation. Even corporations that are currently 'competitors' can be considered in the analysis to be potential stakeholders to generate a new perspective which could be fruitful in opening a dialogue about possible cooperation thus reducing the intensity of competition.

SUMMARY

In summary, the output from the stakeholder analysis is likely to include:

- A completed Power/Interest matrix;
- An analysis of the largest shareholders including their objectives and timescale;
- Full analyses of the stakeholders in Quadrant 1 of the Power/ Interest matrix;
- Selective analysis of other stakeholders picking out observations of strategic significance.

STRATEGIC OPTIONS

Strategy is a framework of dilemmas.

Part III builds on the wide-ranging strategic appraisal covered in Part II to identify possible strategies. Generating strategic options moves the analysis forward from logical analysis of factors to the construction of possible strategic responses. There can never be a single perfect strategy derived from the strategic appraisal. To believe this might be possible would be a dangerous delusion placing the corporate strategist in a god-like position believing that everything can be orchestrated and controlled. In reality there is much that is beyond the corporation's control. The art of option formulation is to provide strategy that is clear and coherent so as to be able to provide the context and direction for decisions taken throughout the corporation at every level, despite the complexity and uncertainty.

A good strategic option may incorporate dilemmas such as: 'flexible' sitting alongside 'focussed'; 'tightly control' alongside 'greater autonomy'; and 'competition' hand-in-hand with 'cooperation'. A good strategy incorporates the inherent contradictions of business life, placing the corporation in a position to respond to whatever happens in the macro business environment.

The analysis up to this point provides sufficient input to formulate strategic options. Part I provided the context with insights into a changing world. The methodology presented in Part II showed how to carry out a strategic appraisal drawing out and distilling factors of significance. Here in Part III, a methodology is presented for building strategic options that capture and makes sense of the dilemmas which executives and managers face, providing consistency of thought in a complex changing world. The process can be summarized by four questions covered in Chapters 11–14: 'Why?', 'On what basis?', 'Where?', and 'How?' using the structure shown in Figure P3.1.

Figure P3.1   Structure Part III

Corporations that answer these questions according to the challenges of the current era will dominate the new business landscape. The answers to these questions lead to a small number of fully-configured strategic options. Part III concludes with Chapter 15, which presents a method to analyse and compare the strategic options in a succinct format to support the process of strategy selection.

CHAPTER 11

DEFINE THE CORPORATE FOOTPRINT

Developing strategy can be thought of as shifting or expanding the corporate footprint.

The starting point to formulate possible strategic options is to ask why the corporation exists. Where to position the footprint of the corporation in the economy and society? Why is the corporation in business? Making money is a requirement, of course, but setting cash or income targets is not strategy. Management through financial targets, although common at the operational level, only works for short-time horizons if deployed at the strategic level as this leads to hollowing out the corporation and is likely to lead to its demise. Consistent profitability arises as a by-product of a higher purpose.

Using the input from the strategic appraisal there should be sufficient depth and breadth of strategic insight to clarify and finalize a statement of core purpose. This becomes the foundation of the strategy. The detailed formulation of strategy can add further insights which may refine the core purpose but this needs to be subject to a robust analysis to ensure that such change comes from deep insight rather than simple convenience.

In this chapter, strategy is visualized as occupying a footprint in the business landscape. Developing strategy can be thought of as a process of shifting or expanding this corporate footprint to a space where the corporation can stand apart from its competitors. Three concepts of strategic space are introduced. First is the Prime Opportunity Space (POS) at the interface between government objectives and customers' needs where industry is not providing what is required, or not doing it very well. If a space can be identified here, it could be a good strategy to replant the corporate footprint here before other corporations move in to exploit the opportunity. Second is the Unique Competing Space (UCS) where the corporation dominates and third is the Shared Operating Space (SOS) where the corporation has activities in collaboration with other corporations. When insights through these different lenses are brought together they help define the strategic footprint that defines the nature and shape of the strategy but first we need to revisit the core purpose.

CORE PURPOSE

A core purpose statement should have been drafted before carrying out the strategic appraisal to give direction to the analysis (Chapter 5). After the strategic appraisal has been completed, it should be possible to confirm whether or not this core statement of purpose continues to be appropriate. The discussion around the detailed wording, in the light of the appraisal, can draw out useful insights to tie down why the corporation exists and define its line of business.

Formulating, and later promulgating, an inspiring and clear statement of purpose provides clarity to executives, workers, customers and investors (Box 11.1). People tend to be cynical of such corporate statements but if a corporation can live up to its stated aspirations it can generate strategic value through:

- Gaining the trust of customers;
- Reinforcing the commitment of staff;
- Winning increased freedom to operate; and
- Generating stable and reliable income streams.

In defining the core business, the strategist should be thinking about identifying a unique space within the business landscape. Being the mirror of another corporation is a recipe for price wars and mutual destruction with no other factor to differentiate products or services except through price. Before planting the corporate footprint

---

BOX 11.1 EXAMPLES OF CORE PURPOSE STATEMENTS

Shell[1]

'Our strategy seeks to reinforce our position as a leader in the oil and gas industry while helping to meet global energy demand in a responsible way.'

Walmart[2]

'Saving people money so they can live better.'

Ecotricity[3]

'Our mission is to change the way electricity is made and used in Britain.'

---

1 http://www.shell.com/global/aboutshell/our-strategy.html [accessed 13 Nov 2013].
2 http://corporate.walmart.com/our-story/ [accessed 13 Nov 2013].
3 http://www.ecotricity.co.uk/about-ecotricity [accessed 13 Nov 2013].

into the business landscape, the core purpose statement provides context and guidance but, paradoxically, nothing is excluded from consideration as strategic options are developed; including the possibility of transformational change to pursue opportunities identified in the POS.

THE PRIME OPPORTUNITY SPACE (POS)

The concept of the Prime Opportunity Space is a way to encourage thinking outside the constraints of the corporation's current footprint when considering future strategy. Figure 11.1 shows the intersection between 'customer needs', 'industry capabilities' and 'government priorities'.

The footprint of the corporation is not shown here, as this is a strategic choice yet to be made. Areas of government policy, not currently of direct interest to the corporation could be brought into the frame. Despite encouraging unconstrained thinking, it would be sensible that the analysis has roots in the activities and capabilities at which the corporation currently excels. The prime opportunities are in areas where the government has set, or is likely to set, priorities and enact legislation which require customer needs to change and which currently industry is not able to deliver. A recent example is renewable energy technology. Future examples may be the technology and capabilities required to deliver efficient and cost-effective closed lifecycle production systems.

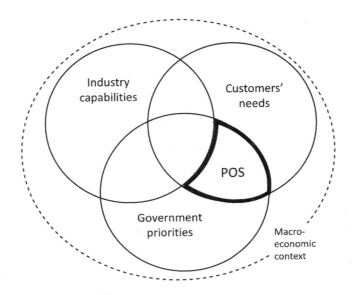

Figure 11.1   Prime Opportunity Space (POS)

The POS is used as a trigger to think strategically and long-term about transformational change. Such strategic options carry risk but these risks can be mitigated by the nature of the opportunities identified. The corporation would be entering a commercial environment without mature competitors and, because there is close alignment with governmental priorities, it is likely there will be opportunities to bid for government grants and exploit government incentives. These commercial dynamics are very attractive so eventually the industry will wake up to the possibilities, at which point there will be other companies chasing the same opportunities. To get ahead of the pack, the strategic thinking needs clear foresight so that the corporation can be staking its claim to the POS before the opportunity has been established, before government has introduced legislation and well before customers have even thought about how their needs will change (For an example of the strategic insight that the concept of the POS can generate see Box 11.2).

BOX 11.2 WIND TURBINE POS

In the 1980s, the Danish government enacted a political vision to capitalize on the country's wind power potential and place the country at the forefront of the wind energy business. The seeds had been planted in the late 1970s with government sponsored R&D at the leading edge of turbine design which helped to establish the three-bladed wind turbine as the standard design for wind energy generation. The government developed a policy package that included consistent financial support mechanisms and priority grid access to give investors the confidence to build turbines on a commercial basis. Denmark is now home to a EUR 6.6 billion wind turbine industry and in 2012 generated 27 per cent of its electricity from wind (EWEA 2013). The Ministry of Foreign Affairs of Denmark claims that 'Danish manufacturers produced turbines, foundations and installations for 90 percent of the world's accumulated offshore wind power in 2011' (Ministry of Foreign Affairs of Denmark 2013).

The Danish government action came well before wind turbine manufacturing was generally commercially viable. The Danish companies that accepted the challenge are now world leading manufacturers of wind turbines. The Danish government can take much of the credit but nothing would have happened unless there were engineering companies willing to take the bold strategic decision to work with the government's vision at a time when wind energy was not in vogue.

The POS has explored the possibility of a big strategic leap into new areas. The POS is used to explore the possibility of a big strategic leap into new areas.

Bringing the analysis closer to home, the interface between customers and the firm is of course strategically important. The intersection between the corporation's capabilities and customers' needs is where the corporation has solid roots in the current industry and is already delivering what customers need (Figure 11.2 overleaf).

Examination of this strategic space is about expanding and shifting the current corporate footprint and carries less risk than the transformational strategies arising out of the POS.

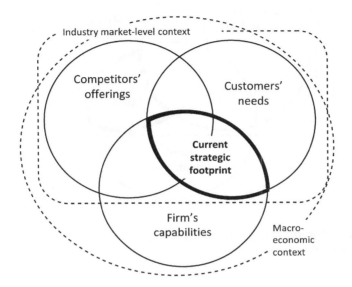

Figure 11.2   Current strategic footprint

UNIQUE COMPETING SPACE (UCS)

The strategic space between the 'corporation's capabilities' and 'customers' needs' can be subdivided into a space where competition rules (the UCS) and a space dominated by cooperation (the SOS). Through the lens of competition, the UCS will be examined drawing on the work of George Tovstiga (2010) before going on to use the lens of cooperation to examine the SOS.

The UCS is where the corporation is delivering products or services in ways that competitors cannot. A small or reducing UCS is a sign of trouble ahead; strategy should aim to defend and expand the competitive footprint making maximum use of existing strengths and capabilities.

The competitor interface labelled '1' defines what differentiates the organization from its competitors. There is a tension across this interface as competitors attempt to encroach on the corporation's territory and strategy needs to define how the corporation will resist. The customer interface is labelled '2'. This represents where evolving customer needs can be identified and brought inside the corporation's

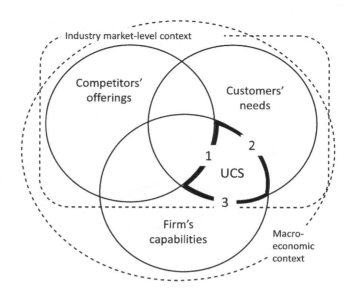

Figure 11.3   Unique Competing Space (UCS)
Source: Adapted from Tovstiga (2010)

value proposition. The internal resource mobilization interface is labelled '3'. This represents the process of bringing together the corporation's resources and capabilities to deliver what customers need. The effectiveness of this process is a key component of the corporation's ability to compete.

Using the UCS focusses the footprint analysis on three distinct aspects of corporate competitive performance. Considering the competitor interface (1) focusses thinking on how to prevent other corporations impinging on the UCS with measures such as securing intellectual property. Examining the customer interface (2) initiates thinking through changing and evolving customer needs and how the corporation can satisfy them, and is fundamental to selling the corporation's products and services. Probing the internal interface (3) sparks ideas to improve the mobilization of corporate resources which is an important aspect of competitive advantage. Considering these three interfaces provides different angles on the strategic challenge of maintaining a strong UCS.

The UCS is a useful way to visualize and define the specific space the corporation occupies within the competitive corporate landscape but the UCS alone is insufficient to capture the more nuanced strategies of the twenty-first century corporate world.

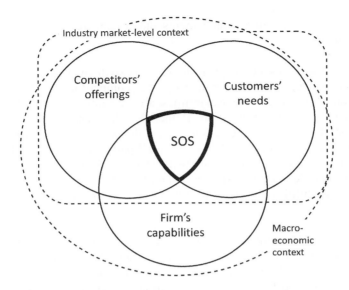

Figure 11.4   Shared Operating Space (SOS)

SHARED OPERATING SPACE (SOS)

The counterpart to the UCS is the SOS.

The SOS is potentially ultra-competitive where other corporations also operate and adopting a narrow competitive view is likely to lead to competition on price and reduced profitability. This is why the corporate focus within the SOS should be on strategic cooperation to build solid and sustainable lines of business. The interface with competitors behaves like a semi-permeable membrane. As well as pushing back against competitors to prevent them crossing into the corporation's UCS, the strategic thinking around exploiting the SOS is driven by exploring the possibilities of cooperation. You want to keep your competitors at bay but you are happy to feed capabilities into the SOS in support of joint ventures. The interface between the SOS and other competitors is where they will seek to provide their capabilities into the SOS. The corporation can utilize these where they are the best value. The strategic intention is two-fold: to secure control over generic industry capabilities through cooperative arrangements; and develop lines of business that meld the best of other corporate capabilities with the corporation's own expertise. Operating in the SOS requires negotiation of a balance between that which the corporation takes and that which it gives back through increased industry efficiency in ways that suits all parties. Note that pushing beyond the boundaries of the SOS into other corporation's UCS will not be welcome and should be used with full knowledge that such action could unravel existing cooperative arrangements and destabilize lines of business that reside in the SOS.

Using the SOS focusses the footprint analysis on two distinct aspects of corporate cooperative strategy. First, considering the competitor interface focusses thinking on which corporate capabilities are currently leading the industry but are at risk of commoditization. Rather than let this descend into a price competition, the strategy could seek to cement the corporation's capability as the industry standard in a venture delivering to all parties at arm's length from the corporation. Second, examination of the interfaces with other corporations could lead to consideration of joint ventures that pull together corporate resources with competitor capabilities to deliver common products or services efficiently and profitably.

Exploiting the SOS requires dialogue with competitors to find efficient ways to cooperate to mutual advantage. This might entail the use of joint ventures to ensure fair, open and honest business dealing. Instead of competing head-to-head, strategy should focus on the negotiation of cooperative business models that deliver efficient solutions to what society needs in ways the government would support. In this way corporations can avoid complaints of anti-competitive behaviour while building stable secure lines of business complementary to their core offering.

CONCLUSION

The output from defining the corporate footprint is a clarified statement of core purpose together with some detail on how the corporation interacts with the wider economy and society. Where the parameters from the three views provided by considering the POS, UCS and SOS are consistent there may be one clear unambiguous footprint that will be common to all the strategic options that are subsequently developed. Alternatively, the analysis could identify a range of footprints which may become the basis of radically different strategic options. These strategic footprints may be described in whatever way seems appropriate which could be as a collection of objectives sitting below the core purpose.

SUMMARY

Strategy can be visualized as the footprint the corporation occupies in the business landscape consistent with the core purpose of the corporation. Developing strategy can be thought of as a process of shifting or expanding this corporate footprint to a place where the corporation is secure and can thrive. The three concepts presented here to support developing the corporate footprint are:

Prime Opportunity Space (POS) focussed on future opportunities;
Unique Competing Space (UCS) focussed on competition and;
Shared Operating Space (SOS) focussed on building cooperation.

Each model provides a different perspective; all three views are needed to define the strategic footprint of the corporation. There might be one clear unambiguous footprint or a number of different possible footprints underpinning different strategic options.

CHAPTER 12

CORE STRATEGY SELECTION

Strategies which rise above conventional strategic thinking will be the way to build stable and secure corporations fit for the twenty-first century.

Core strategy selection is a complex and potentially confusing activity with conflicting priorities and an infinite number of possibilities. In this sense, the process is a reflection of reality but the resulting strategy has to rise above this complexity to deliver a framework that can be communicated and understood throughout the organization.

In practice, there is a huge amount to be considered but it is suggested here that the core logic is kept simple. The management literature is full of hefty tomes seeking to explain in ever more detail every aspect of strategy. It may keep academics in work but it is of limited practical value. Strategy should not be a game only understood by the 'experts' but a process that fully engages with the real world dealt with by corporate executives and managers.

In this chapter, a structured approach is presented based on straightforward core concepts. The aim is to find a basis for the business that lifts the corporation out of the hypercompetitive space with a strategy that is likely to endure. The first consideration is which generic strategy, low-cost, differentiation or focus would be the best fit. This leads into discussion of two special strategic situations so persuasively good for business that they should be considered before all others: 'Blue Ocean' and 'Civic Monopoly'.

GENERIC STRATEGIES

The classic bedrock of management theory is the framework of generic strategies outlined by Michael Porter (1980).

According to this simple conceptual model, a business has to choose to operate either on the basis of low-cost or differentiation to serve a broad market or a niche market. This leads to four potential generic strategies. Competing on the basis of

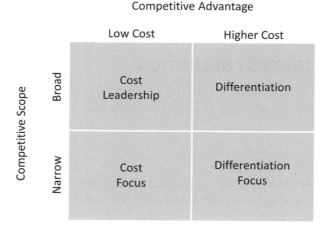

Figure 12.1   Porter's generic strategies

the lowest cost product or service requires the company's operations and supply chain to be squeezed to reduce costs and maximize efficiency. Competing on the basis of differentiation relies on serving customers with what they need better than competitors through careful crafting of a unique offering winning business through a differentiated product or service. Low-cost strategy is tough to deliver because customers who purchase on this basis are fickle customers who will shift to an alternative supplier offering a lower price. This means that choosing to focus on low-cost requires an unrelenting squeeze on costs taking every opportunity to shave the price. Differentiation is more likely to provide the commercial basis that will endure, easing the pressure on the corporation thus allowing a certain amount of resource available for adaptation in a changing world.

FROM THEORY TO REALITY

The classic view of strategy is that the organization should not get stuck in the middle trying to both differentiate and deliver lowest cost. In the words of Michael Porter:

> *The firm stuck in the middle is almost guaranteed low profitability. It either loses the high-volume customers who demand low prices or must bid away its profits to get this business away from low-cost firms. Yet it also loses high-margin businesses – the cream – to the firms who are focused on high-margin targets or have achieved differentiation overall. The firm stuck in the middle also probably suffers from a blurred corporate culture and a conflicting set of organizational arrangements and motivation system. (Porter 1980:41–42)*

The duality of being 'stuck in the middle' confuses the corporation with some parts of the organization driving down costs whilst other parts are focused on increasing customer value. The risk is that costs are not driven to their lowest level and the product or service is not a first-choice product (Box 12.1). 'Stuck in the middle' is neither the best nor the cheapest. This can be a tough sell, so a simple view of strategy is to avoid such a position and select either low-cost or differentiation. This simplification remains good advice to ensure clarity of the core strategy.

In reality, corporations will be running two overlapping cycles of activity, holding costs in check concurrent with delivering what the customer needs, winning business on the basis of 'best value'. Being 'in the middle' may in reality be appropriate but in highly competitive markets this is increasingly tough. The key is not to be 'stuck', through being able and willing to break out of the competitive straightjacket. Two special cases are presented below as 'Blue Ocean' and 'Civic Monopoly'. These are so attractive that the first strategic consideration should be whether it is possible for the corporation to adopt one of these.

BOX 12.1 NOKIA – STUCK IN THE MIDDLE

Through the 1990s, Nokia was the world leader in developing and bringing to a mass market the mobile phone (cell phone). The strategic decision to focus on telecommunications, plus the early investment in GSM, paid off. Between 1996 and 2001, Nokia's turnover increased almost five-fold from EUR 6.5 billion to EUR 31 billion (Nokia 2013). By 1998, Nokia was the world''s largest vendor of mobile phones, a position it retained until 2012 (BBC 2012).

In 2007, a shift in the mobile phone market was taking place as Apple launched the I-Phone and took the market by storm with a phone that was cool. The I-Phone became the must-have phone putting Apple in the strong strategic position of the phone of choice where sales were not price sensitive. If you wanted to be seen with the coolest phone it had to be Apple. This was not just clever marketing but astute strategy reading the shift in the market where the technology was becoming commoditized and the differentiation would now be on features and style.

Nokia responded with ever better phones for the top-end of the market as well as cheap phones for the low-end of the market (particularly in developing markets). However, Nokia was no longer customers' first choice and was also struggling to compete on price with the commodity phone manufacturers. In 2013, Nokia was still shifting a lot of phones and remained a going concern but being 'stuck in the middle' put the corporation in the eye of the competitive storm where small mistakes are punished by the market.

The Nokia share price reached a nadir of $2 in June 2013 compared with over $35 in 2007. The management finally through in the towel and sold its mobile phone business to Microsoft for 5.4 bn euros ($7.2 bn; £4.5 bn) (BBC 2013a).

BLUE OCEAN

When the article 'Blue Ocean Strategy' appeared in Harvard Business Review in 2004 it was a revelation. Out of the turgid world of management theory here was something really useful, simple to visualize and close to reality. The commercial world was likened to an ocean full of competing corporations swimming around fighting each other for business resulting in blood in the water, hence the concept of a 'Red Ocean'. This is not an easy place to operate where there is always the need to push hard to win and retain business. The better place to operate is in a 'Blue Ocean'. In the article this was defined as 'all the industries not in existence today – the unknown market space, untainted by competition' (Kim and Mauborgne 2004:77). The Blue Ocean arises from opening up a new space in the commercial landscape which does not yet exist and where there are no competitors. Finding and entering such a space allows the corporation to swim free to exploit the new opportunities unencumbered by competition (Box 12.2).

The simple analogy of the Blue Ocean had such resonance with me when it was published because of my work at the time on sustainability as a key driver of strategy. The image of a pristine clean ocean to replace the old industrialized strategies of the past was compelling. This perspective may not have been what the authors intended but it served my purpose to place the ideas of sustainability into a solid strategic framework. Society, the economy and business is locked into a Red Ocean where small marginal changes will have very little effect. We have to make the leap into a Blue Ocean, where if you can swim it is a great place to be, but it you are laden down with out-of-date processes and old technology you will sink like a stone. My book

---

BOX 12.2 BLUE OCEAN EXAMPLES

Two examples explained by Kim and Mauborgne (2005):

Cirque du Soleil

Cirque du Soleil created a new, highly-profitable market within the ailing circus industry. The traditional circus model was overturned taking out the cost drivers of animals and individual star performers and bringing in elements from opera and ballet. The result was a totally new entertainment concept for a new adult audience.

The Body Shop

The Body Shop created a 'Blue Ocean' in the fiercely competitive cosmetics industry. The strategy eschewed most glamorous aspects of the industry, instead building an image around functionality, reduced prices and modest packaging. Increased value was given to natural ingredients, a healthy lifestyle and ethical concerns. As a result The Body Shop's products appealed to a totally new group of customers and achieved a high degree of cost savings in an industry where a large proportion of costs arise from packaging and advertizing.

Adapt and Thrive : The Sustainable Revolution (2008) charted a route to navigate successfully into the blue ocean of opportunities that arise when the world wakes up to the need for sustainability. It is interesting that at the time of writing many of the opportunities outlined have still not been fully exploited. It is as if corporations, society and government are waiting for the starting gun. Certainly the corporations who have made the early seed investments are poised to reap their rewards but the fact that sustainability is such a slow fuse does not mean the explosion of opportunities will be any less impressive when it comes.

The Blue Ocean is indisputably a good place to pitch strategy. If Blue Oceans were obvious there would already be corporations vying to fill them but, by their nature, Blue Oceans are non-obvious and may need to be created. Constructing a blue ocean strategy may require manipulation beyond the confines of the corporation to set the circumstances to make the new business viable. It may require change in attitudes in society or change to government legislation to open up the channel that leads to a Blue Ocean. It is worth expending considerable thought and analysis to examine if there is a viable Blue Ocean for the corporation because, if this is possible, it lifts the corporation out of the maelstrom of competition to a place where it can navigate unimpeded.

This leads on to the other attractive strategic space, the Civic Monopoly.

CIVIC MONOPOLY

There are some parts of the economy which by their nature are monopolies such as water supply, electricity and railways. Operating such activities effectively and efficiently requires good management according to sound commercial parameters. Public ownership can lead to inefficiency brought about by a lack of commercial discipline; private ownership can lead to inefficiency due to the bureaucratic process of pseudo-competition. The middle way is the concept of a 'Civic Monopoly' defined as:

> *A natural monopoly which needs to be managed with commercial discipline*
> *for the benefit of wider society.*

Having a monopoly is of course a great strategy – where you can get away with it. Legal ways to build a monopoly are through patent or a quasi-monopoly built on brand. The natural monopoly provided by a Civic Monopoly is also attractive to business but governments will be wary of increasing corporate freedom in this area. As society transitions to more sustainable ways of operating, and business demonstrates that it can be trusted, the range of possible civic monopolies is likely to increase. For example, energy supply can be delivered more efficiently (in an engineering and low-carbon sense) through coordinated local arrangements making best use of the community's renewable energy opportunities orchestrated by Energy Service Companies (ESCOs) (Box 12.3).

BOX 12.3 ENERGY SERVICE COMPANIES (ESCOS)

In the current model of energy supply, demand and supply are dealt with on a linear basis. Rising demand leads to building more power stations. This is wasteful but deeply engrained commercial behaviour which could operate while fossil fuel is cheap and plentiful. This linear model breaks down as the economy moves beyond fossil fuel. Part of the solution is Energy Service Companies (ESCOs) covering a range of activities to operate the new circular model of balancing demand with renewable capacity. The transition is slowly taking place but it will be some time before the new parameters are understood and implemented (London Energy Partnership 2007).

ESCOs can deal with every aspect of the energy demand and use cycle:

- Investment in insulation and energy efficiency measures;
- Involvement in the planning process to facilitate low-carbon infrastructure;
- Combined heat and power units embedded in communities at building or district level;
- Community renewable energy projects such as wind turbines (allowed by the local community because they are operated for the local community);
- Collective arrangements to drive investment in solar panels on all suitable roofs.

ESCOs are natural civic monopolies which will become widespread. The existing power corporations are slow to work out the strategic implications; they should regard this as a huge opportunity rather than a threat.

Over recent years the approach taken by the UK government – and in many other countries – is to privatize public utilities in tandem with introducing competition. The elements of competition are highly artificial but it approximates to the economic model of a competitive market. When such pseudo markets are established the interests of society and the government are usually represented by the appointment of a regulator.

The concept of privatization came to prominence in the UK in the 1980s when the government of the day took the view that the unions had disproportionate power and bureaucratic rules and inefficiency in the public sector was rife. Privatization has indeed taken power away from unions and brought a semblance of commercial discipline but the search for economic efficiency has introduced a whole raft of real-world inefficiencies. Railways provide an interesting example of the consequences of privatization. In 1991 EU Directive 91/440 made it a legal requirement for independent companies to be able to apply for non-discriminatory track access on a European Union country's track. The British government was keen to embrace full privatization leading to the UK model of railway provision (Box 12.4).

BOX 12.4 THE PRIVATIZATION OF BRITISH RAIL

The Privatization of British Rail in 1993 sold the network into private ownership structured as a rail infrastructure company, RailTrack and numerous operating companies each contracted to run specific routes. There have been a number of improvements including less disruption caused by union action and trains generally run to time but the overall objectives of the privatization have failed. In particular there has been a net increase of £1.7bn in Government subsidy between 1996/97 and 2009/10 (Department for Transport 2011).

The situation after two decades of privatization is that public subsidy has increased and huge inefficiencies arise such as piecemeal procurement of rolling stock. Through complex legal arrangements, a pseudo-market operates with the train operating companies and the government regulators locked in conflict such as the dispute with Virgin Trains over the West Coast Main Line (*Railnews* 2012). The Department for Transport and the Office of Rail Regulation (ORR) are struggling to find ways to make the UK rail industry efficient and responsive to the users' needs whilst reducing the drain on government funds (Department for Transport 2011).

Investing in rail is a growing priority at a time when the UK needs to reduce carbon emissions – as low-carbon rail is relatively easy to implement – but the current arrangements in the UK are holding the industry back. Privatization according to the UK template developed in the 1990s is no longer working to deliver the objectives of society and government.

The flaws in the structure adopted for UK railways have become evident over the two decades since privatization. There are too many resources expended managing the market; as the corporations work out how to get around the regulator to maximize profits and the regulator struggles to control the industry for the public good. Privatization has been useful to introduce a more commercial approach into UK rail operations but after taking the easy efficiency gains the pseudo-market model no longer looks fits for purpose. The time has come to move forward with the concept of well-run civic monopolies.

The concept of civic monopolies is not a reversion to public ownership (although that is one way) but a move forward to a true collaboration between society, government and business. As governments start to understand the potential, a huge opportunity opens up for business. Where a natural monopoly exists (or can be created) it should be run as a civic monopoly. A key issue is ownership; not public or private but an ownership model that draws in a range of stakeholders. Allowing a civic monopoly is better than both public ownership and an improvement on the pseudo-market established through privatization. Finland responded to the EU requirement that railways should be managed by independent companies with a structure much better suited to serving its stakeholders (Box 12.5). Although Finnish rail is ultimately publicly owned, the structure allows for commercial freedom and commercial discipline at arms-length from government without resorting to privatization.

The UK and Finnish experience of putting rail onto a commercial basis shows striking differences. The use of competition theory in the UK has established a for-profit industry competing against a regulator; in Finland the industry has been set up to align control directly with stakeholder interests. The results would indicate that the Finnish cultural approach of shared responsibility has been more effective in this case than privatization but what are the lessons for corporate strategy? What is a civic monopoly and how should it operate?

BOX 12.5 THE COMMERCIALIZATION OF FINNISH RAIL

In 1990 Finnish State Railways ceased to be a civil service department and became a public enterprise, and five years later a state-owned limited liability company. VR-Group Ltd, a limited liability company owned entirely by the Finnish state, with its subsidiaries was incorporated on 1 July 1995. VR Group describes itself thus:

VR Group is an ecofriendly, versatile company with responsible operations offering transport, logistics and infrastructure engineering services. (VR Group 2013)

VR Group is one hundred per cent owned by the Finnish State and comprises three business divisions that operate around customer segments. These are: VR, providing passenger services; VR Transpoint, providing logistics services; and VR Track, specializing in infrastructure engineering. The Group's head office is in Helsinki and it operates mainly in Finland but it also has operations abroad, especially in Russia and Sweden. VR Group contains altogether 23 companies and has eight associated companies. VR Group's net turnover in 2012 totalled EUR 1,437.8 million. In addition to the members of the Board of Directors, who are responsible for managing the business, there is a Supervisory Board which includes Members of Parliament and Union representatives.

The Finnish government have established VR Group with the freedom and responsibility to run its affairs on a commercial basis without civil service interference but by retaining state ownership it can be run in the way that suits a civic monopoly:

VR Group plays an important social role in Finland. The Group carries responsibility for its economic vitality and for the impacts of it operations on the environment and on society more generally. (VR Group Annual Report 2012)

This structure works because of the responsible attitude adopted by the management team and the trust placed by government. This stable secure corporate structure relies on the management to continually seek to improve performance and efficiency to deliver the public good of an efficient rail network. The amorphous quality of 'responsibility' is used in place of the blunt hammer of forced competition.

The commercial parameters of operating within a civic monopoly are to deliver quality and efficiency adding up to value for society. The business should make a profit, of course, but this should be fair and transparent. To be able to adopt such a core strategy the corporation needs to address ownership issues (covered in the next chapter) in order to craft a fully configured and workable strategic option. The idea of relinquishing ownership (fully or partly) may ring alarm bells in many corporate headquarters bringing a halt to further analysis but this would be short-sighted. The strategy process should consider whether a civic monopoly is appropriate and take the idea through to working how it could be done, even if it is later rejected due to, for example, shareholder concerns.

A new civic monopoly could be completely unregulated, and remain unregulated, if the commercial players behave in a transparent and responsible manner. An existing monopoly is likely to be highly regulated so there will need to be transitional arrangements, including setting objectives and priorities concurrent with acceptance of the principle that voluntary compliance is more effective than the burden of regulation. Regulations need to exist but dogmatic enforcement should be avoided. The ideal position is where the regulator aspires to zero-enforcement and may even cease to exist. The business should be free to evolve the way it operates as circumstances change with regulator or government stepping in only when and where required.

The way civic monopolies are likely to evolve is that considerable regulatory power remains on the statute books but considerable latitude is used to judge what constitutes efficient delivery of public good according to a general principle of non-interference. This would not be possible working inside the current corporate norms, but if business recognizes the advantages and mirrors the role of government by adopting transparently responsible behaviour, civic monopolies could become commonplace. Government will not lead for fear of being hoodwinked by powerful corporate interests, so business should lead by championing more responsible strategy to start the virtuous circle of a new wave of de-regulation.

The concept of enlightened government working in tandem with enlightened corporations looks like a pipedream in today's corporate world but the attractions of such mutual advantage are strong. For management the attraction is increased freedom to make the right decisions without interference; for government the attraction is improved services and the prospect of less public subsidy. As regulation is ratcheted down, and corporations adjust strategy and structure in response, civic monopolies will emerge which have the trust of government and considerable freedom to operate.

SUMMARY

Core strategy selection defines the commercial basis on which the strategy is built. The classic theory of competitive advantage leads to considering which generic strategy to select: low-cost or differentiation (see Figure 12.1). Before making this choice, it should be considered whether it is possible to break out of the competitive business environment into a Blue Ocean or a Civic Monopoly. The freedom to operate that these provide is so attractive that it is worth trying to construct such candidate strategic options for consideration. The process is worth doing, even if it is felt that there is little chance in the current corporate climate to convince either board members or shareholders to take such a fundamental change of direction. Shifting to core strategies which rise above the standard generic strategies will be the way to build stable and secure corporations fit for the twenty-first century but it will take time for the ideas to embed. The following decision-tree is proposed:

1. Is there a Blue Ocean the corporation can sail into? This is the best strategy, and worth a long hard search, but such opportunities are rare.
2. Is there a civic monopoly opportunity? This is potentially a good core strategy but has implications for the ownership structure of the corporation.
3. If neither 1 nor 2 apply, the corporation remains in the highly competitive mainstream business environment and must decide which of the generic strategies to adopt of low-cost or differentiation.

CHAPTER 13

MARKETS AND LOCATIONS

Where to sell; where to make; where to orchestrate.

By this stage of the analysis, it is likely that some implicit assumptions have already been made about the markets to target and the location of operations. These assumptions need to be put aside to ensure the aperture of analysis is wide open to the emerging possibilities. The drive towards globalized solutions has been effective in recent years in delivering quick wins but it is now becoming clear that this can destroy corporate value over the longer term – and no longer suited to the emerging political and economic landscape. The 'where' question now leads to very different answers compared with an analysis made during the years when economic globalization dominated policy.

The question 'where to sell', breaks down into an analysis of whether to sell new products (or services) to existing markets or existing products to new markets or jump ahead to new products in new markets. The question 'where to make' leads to considering the best geographic location for production and operations, bearing in mind that the rationale can alter quickly as factors beyond the corporation's control change the logic. One such change is the shift in favour of production close to markets due to concerns about supply-chain risk, political resistance to globalization and the increasing cost of transportation. The question 'where to orchestrate' arises as the focus shifts to short supply chains and increasing local and regional autonomy.

MARKETS AND PRODUCTS

A simple and effective tool to analyse markets and products is the Product/Market Expansion Grid often referred to by the name of its originator as the Ansoff matrix (Ansoff 1957). This remains a staple tool of strategic analysis and useful for considering growth options(see Figure 13.1 overleaf).

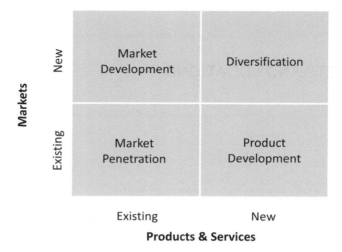

Figure 13.1   Product/market expansion grid

Each quadrant represents an option to consider:

- *Market Development*: Seek to sell existing products to new markets leveraging brand and reputation;
- *Product Development*: Seek to sell new products to existing markets utilizing corporate capabilities to develop new and better products;
- *Diversification*: Seek to sell new products to new markets where high returns justify the risk; and
- *Market Penetration*: Seek to sell existing products to existing markets in greater quantity and/or with higher margins.

This framework is useful to trigger thinking and specificity comes from selecting the preferred quadrant which then becomes another building block of the strategy.

PRODUCTION OPERATIONS

International business has been dominated for many years by outsourcing and offshoring in a relentless search for lowest cost of production. Locating production in the lowest cost locations is a fluid puzzle as relative country advantage shifts. In the period after China joined the WTO in 2001, China became a favoured destination but as labour costs have risen other countries like Vietnam have taken the mantle of lowest cost. However the fashion for off-shoring is waning as corporations have built up experience of the long-term consequences. The initial business case may have been persuasive but the on-going management of remote production has in many cases become a problem. One factor is reputation; it is no longer acceptable to shift production to where labour costs are cheap and regulations less onerous while remaining blind to the consequences for the workers and the environment. Of more direct commercial interest, a number of problems have arisen from shifting production away from close corporate oversight including loss of in-house expertise, leakage of intellectual property, less agility to respond to changing customer needs and increased supply chain risk.

SUPPLY CHAIN RISK

The disaster at Fukushima exposed the reality that long supply chains are risky (Box 13.1). For many years the theoretical benefits of sourcing from the cheapest location (best price/quality balance) according to lean supply chains working to the principle of just-in-time had ruled strategic thinking. The risks were obvious – to anyone thinking through the analysis – but the figures from computing the efficiencies and cost savings were so good that it seemed like a no-brainer. Just so, this was a prime example of a lack of brains. Strategy driven by the analysis of spread sheets and calculations of ROI seemed to make people blind to the obvious realities. Supply chain strategy is a prime example where concepts should be developed with a big dose of common sense and the accountants kept out of the room until a later stage to put numbers to what are judged to be viable and resilient options. There is no point in conceptualizing a supply chain based on maximum economic efficiency if all you are doing is building a house of cards.

BOX 13.1 FUKUSHIMA, JAPAN

The Fukushima Daiichi Nuclear Power Plant, consisting of six boiling water reactors, was overwhelmed by a tsunami on 11 March 2011 knocking out power supplies for the cooling systems. It was a well maintained plant which had shut down correctly and automatically when the earthquake struck but the resulting wall of water 50 minutes later breached the 10m sea wall protection. The rooms where the emergency generators are housed were flooded and the generators failed, closing down power to the primary cooling system. Secondary cooling systems running on emergency battery power continued to circulate cooling water until the next day when they too failed. Two of the reactors were in cold shutdown for maintenance and were safe but the residual heat in the other reactors built up to the point where the fuel rods began to melt and explosive gases built up leading to a series of explosions. This was the world's worst nuclear accident since Chernobyl 1986 and will require huge ongoing clear-up operations that will last for decades.

At the time of the disaster, about 22 per cent of the world's 300mm silicon wafer supply and 60 per cent of critical auto parts were manufactured at plant in the Fukushima prefecture (Fisher 2011). Corporations with highly optimized supply chains reliant on particular suppliers in the vicinity were left exposed when the disaster hit.

While supply chains are running smoothly questioning their resilience is not welcome but there are three prime risks that have to be factored into the analysis:

Reputation

The whole corporate supply chain is seen as within the sphere of the corporation so anything that occurs can reflect back on the corporation.

News channels operate continuously fed by satellite communication to every corner of the globe. The corporation's supply chain may be hidden amongst the back streets of Delhi, or remote factories in China, when it is operating smoothly but as soon as there is a disaster it will be headline news. This was the situation in 2013 when a factory in Bangladesh collapsed putting a number of western retailers in the spotlight (Box 13.2). Whether the corporation is culpable in a legal sense is not particularly relevant; the damage to reputation is done. Trying to argue that the factories, where the corporation's products or components are made, belong to contractors operating at arm's length is no defence from an investigative journalist with a nose for a good story. Where there is exploitation of child labour, lax environmental controls, dreadful working conditions or dangerous factories, anywhere in the supply chain, these are waiting to be exposed. Managing long supply chains to low-cost production centres is like holding a hand grenade with the pin out; one slip up and there can be an explosion of damaging negative press coverage.

Cost of Transport

The current transport system relies almost entirely on oil. While oil is cheap, transport is cheap but the cost of transport will inevitably rise as oil prices rise, coupled with governments increasing taxes to drive down carbon dioxide emissions. It is intuitively correct that dismantling global supply chains is part

---

BOX 13.2 BANGLADESH FACTORY COLLAPSE

On 24 April 2013, the eight-storey Rana Plaza building in the suburbs of Dhaka, collapsed injuring about 2,500 and killing over 1,000 people. Above the bank and shops on the ground and first floors, were five garment factories supplying well-known brands including Primark and Benetton (BBC 2013b). Just a day before the collapse, the building was briefly evacuated when cracks appeared in the walls. However, workers were later allowed back in or told to return to work by the factory owners. The incident was broadcast around the world and dominated world news for days. The owner of the building and the owners of the businesses operating there were blamed for lax safety and ignoring warnings but the negative reaction also extended to the brands which were being supplied.

of building a more sustainable world economy. The commercial reality is that transport is far cheaper than it ought to be. Simple commercial logic will drive change as transport costs rise to a sustainable level. There will be low-carbon transportation, such as high-tech sailing ships, but no one should expect it to be cheap. Supply chains should be evaluated, not on the assumption that artificially cheap transportation will continue, but on the assumption that more realistic costs will apply in the future.

Unexpected Events

> *...we will need systems that don't fall apart when we make a mistake.*
> *(Taleb 2012:125)*

Unexpected and hard-to-predict events of large magnitude have been described as Black Swans by the statistician Nassim Taleb (Taleb 2007). Simple strategic thinking may accept that it is impossible to plan for the unexpected but, as Taleb explains, Black Swan events can depend on the observer. His example is that what may be a Black Swan surprise for a turkey is not a Black Swan surprise to the butcher; hence the objective should be to avoid being the turkey. There are two important observations to help secure this objective.

First, with hindsight, many unexpected events look entirely predictable but care is needed as the rationale may be little more than assembling convenient evidence after the fact. An example of this is the 2008 financial crisis. Many accounts of the crisis cite the United States sub-prime housing market as the cause. It is argued here that it would be wrong to suppose that the exact sequence of events could have been predicted but the fact that the global financial system was highly unstable was clear to see. I wrote and published before the crisis a commentary on the consequences of the high degree of global economic interdependence that had not been seen before (McManners 2008:172). I posed the question: 'is the world financial system a robust self-regulating system or a house of cards waiting to collapse?' I went on to argue that global finance has become a 'system in which we all either stand or fall together ... if collapse does come, there will be no hiding from the consequences'. I could not predict that the US sub-prime mortgage market would be the trigger but logical analysis showed that any failure would compound into a global financial crisis. The systemic global financial problems made a financial crisis inevitable; the only unknown was the timing and the precise trigger event.

Second, truly unpredictable events, like Fukushima, can have entirely predictable consequences. There will always be unexpected events so although we do not know what they will be, we know they will occur. The strategic defence against unexpected events is through evaluation of resilience. Such analysis shows that lean, long supply chains without built-in redundancy carry a high risk. It cannot be predicted where they will fail but it is obvious that such supply chains will suffer occasional massive disruption even though the point of failure cannot be predetermined. From the strategic perspective it should be possible to build in resilience to in effect 'expect the unexpected'.

Proximization Effects

The emerging paradigm of proximization (Chapter 3) will lead to greater national autonomy and increased importance of regional trading blocs. The shift is an inevitable consequence of economic globalization coming up against resource limits leading to countries taking back control of their affairs. The reason these changes are so important is that there can be profound implications for corporate strategy. The importance is amplified because, at the time of writing, there are many economists, policy makers and corporate advisors who still hold to the belief that globalization is irreversible, thus making them blind to the consequences.

There is no simple guide to the consequences of proximization but the general consideration for business is the increasing advantage that local businesses will have serving local markets. The opportunities for global corporations become orchestrating such activity. The emphasis shifts towards locally embedded semi-autonomous operations suited to local geography, resources and culture.

CONCLUSION

To construct viable strategic options the 'where to sell' and 'where to make' are important questions. Assumptions that held true in the past should be challenged and decisions taken based on a forward-looking view of the macroeconomic context and realistic analysis of supply chain resilience.

SUMMARY

Adding detail to the strategic options requires answers to questions over markets and locations:

- Where to sell, breaks down into an analysis of whether to sell new products (or services) to existing markets or existing products to new markets or jump ahead to new products in new markets.
- Where to make, leads to considering the best geographic location for production and operations, bearing in mind that the rationale can alter quickly as factors beyond the corporation's control change the logic.
- Where to orchestrate, arises as the focus shifts to short supply chains and increasing local and regional autonomy.

CHAPTER 14

RESOURCING

To make a strategic option viable it is necessary to gather the package of resources required in a structure capable of delivery.

The final stage of completing the configuration of a strategic option is to decide how to gather the resources needed and construct a corporate structure capable of delivery. The aim of this stage is to close off a viable fully-configured strategy with an identified resource plan. It would be expected to complete two or three such candidate strategies to feed forward into the strategic option evaluation. During implementation there will be numerous further challenges but at this stage the strategy team is in the luxurious position of all options open and no avenue closed. This means that innovative and unusual delivery mechanisms can be considered.

In this chapter, organic delivery is discussed first as the most straightforward mechanism. Where the corporation does not have the required resources, other mechanisms can be considered including acquisition, joint venture and other ownership models; each of these has different characteristics. The common strategic factor is the need to gather the required resources within a structure that suits the corporation, its stakeholders and the nature of the business.

ORGANIC DELIVERY

Delivery of the strategy through the organization's own set of resources is the simplest and most easily controlled. Where the corporation has the know-how, capital and capability to deliver the strategy these can be lined up as required. It is worth checking that the strategic thinking has not subconsciously become bounded by the existing set of resources but, provided this is not the case, the resources can be allocated and the internal structure adjusted to assemble the required package of capabilities.

Where the corporation does not have sufficient capital for the candidate strategy, the two main sources of additional funds are debt or equity financing. Using debt incurs interest charges and banks will expect security for the loan. Equity finance is cheaper, raising funds from existing shareholders (if they take up pre-emption rights) or selling shares to new investors. Another financing option is to issue bonds –typically with a fixed interest over a set period; this will require a sales pitch and interest rate to attract investors. With debt financing there is always the danger that the bank may withdraw its support; equity financing may be cheaper but dilutes ownership; and bonds can be an expensive source of funds. The corporate finance team will need to work out the funding package, but for the strategy formulation the key information is whether the capital can be raised by the corporation or whether it will need to look at other ways to structure the business.

In many cases, organic delivery is not feasible because, for example:

- The corporation does not have access to sufficient capital;
- The corporation, acting alone within its own resources, will not have the speed required to exploit the opportunity effectively;
- The corporation lacks the full set of capabilities required;
- The risk is too great and needs to be shared;
- There are significant potential competitors which should be neutralized to ensure success.

Where organic delivery is not possible, other options include, acquisition, Joint Venture, merger and other ownership models:

ACQUISITION

Strategic reasons for acquisition include:

- To obtain resources and capabilities;
- Vertical integration to secure sources of supply or the route to market;
- To neutralize a potential competitor;
- To harvest synergies and deliver economies of scale.

Integrating acquisitions can be challenging as the acquired business is brought inside the corporate fold. There might be cultural issues to deal with, divergent aims to reconcile and problems that were not fully exposed during the stage of 'due diligence'. There will be integration costs but these should have been factored into the decision to acquire and should be less than the expected benefits for the acquisition to proceed. Serial acquirers that have made a strategic choice to develop expertise in acquiring companies, not surprisingly, have a greater success rate.

It is worth noting that acquisition is a common method of financial engineering used to increase revenue or market share to satisfy market expectations for growth. It may also be used to reap the tax advantages of linking a profitable company with one making losses to reduce tax. Such financial engineering motives should not be allowed to distract management away from using sound strategic logic.

JOINT VENTURE

Joint Ventures (JV) are set up by partnering corporations and can be good corporate vehicles to exploit the SOS (Shared Operating Space; See pages 99–100). They are usually set up as separate entities with management independent of the owning corporations and clear aims and objectives agreed at the outset. There are a number of strategic reasons to use a JV:

- To allow a MNC to work with a local corporation to be, and be seen to be, local within a national market;
- To share risks such as development costs or pursue new industry capabilities where the commercial case is not yet proven;
- To increase levels of cooperation (or reduce levels of competition) in key parts of the value chain;
- To test working together as a preliminary stage before considering an acquisition or merger.

MERGER

A merger is a special case of joining two corporations of equal size but these are fraught with difficulties in terms of implementation with success rates often reported as low as 50 per cent. All too often mergers have an element of hubris amongst chief executives wanting to build empires and, unless the strategic rationale is strong, the opinion of this author is that they are best avoided.

Other Ownership Models

Where a potential strategy has been identified that has high value to the wider stakeholder community but investors are lukewarm, the first question to ask is whether it is a viable strategy? Perhaps it is viable but only under an alternative ownership model. This can take strategic thinking towards mobilizing support from the stakeholders likely to benefit. This can be, but does not have to be, financial investment. In a book on corporate strategy, to be read widely within the corporate world, it will seem odd to present alternative ownership models such as foundations, mutual corporations and cooperatives. However to consider such ownership structures is the logical outcome of putting the mantra of shareholder value to one side. There are examples of successful corporations which demonstrate that alternative ownership models can work such as the John Lewis Partnership (Box 14.1) and the Co-operative Group in the UK and the Finnish retailing cooperative organization, S Group.

BOX 14.1 JOHN LEWIS PARTNERSHIP

Rightly or wrongly I feel quite certain that the general idea of substituting partnership for exploiting employment is now-a-days in the air and will spread through industry of all kinds. It is already dear to many hearts besides my own, for it makes work something to live for as well as something to live by. Here may be the new source of working energy of which our country is in such grave need.

John Spedan Lewis (1957)

The Partnership was established in 1929 by John Spedan Lewis and now has over 85,500 Partners who own 40 John Lewis shops (30 department stores and 10 John Lewis at home shops), 302 Waitrose supermarkets, an online and catalogue business - johnlewis.com, a production unit and a farm. All employees are Partners sharing in the benefits and profits of the business.

The Partnership's reputation is founded on the uniqueness of our ownership structure and our commercial success. Our purpose is 'the happiness of all our members, through their worthwhile, satisfying employment in a successful business', with success measured on our ability to sustain and enhance our position both as an outstanding retailer and as a thriving example of employee ownership.

John Lewis Partnership (2013)

It is an understatement that shifting to alternative ownership models may not be liked by existing shareholders with pure financial motives, but they can be bought off if the circumstances are right and the strategic rationale is strong. At the very least, considering alternative ownership models to deliver strategy, can inject novel and interesting strategic options into the mix for consideration. A wave of alternative ownership models for corporations currently listed on the markets should not be expected any time soon but it is possible to start the discussion.

FOUNDATION

The global corporation IKEA is an example where a foundation has been set up to act as the owner of the corporation. This highly successful corporation shows the possibilities that responsible capitalism can deliver (Box 14.2).

Where the ownership is placed in a foundation it is possible for the foundation to influence corporate decisions. The commercial arm of a charity is an example where the owner may have particular objectives beyond the requirement for a financial return. Old-school finance and investment experts can be found seeking to persuade foundations and charities to regard the commercial company's they own as simply machines to generate money for the charity to spend on its objectives. This is a view that responsible trustees and charity directors should

---

BOX 14.2 IKEA

The IKEA Group is a major multinational corporation with total sales of EUR 27 billion ($37 billion), 298 stores in 26 countries, 9,500 products, 139,000 'co-workers' and 1,084 home furnishing suppliers in 53 countries (2012 figures). The founder of IKEA, Ingvar Kamprad, created an ownership structure that ensures the corporation remains independent and can take a long-term approach. Since 1982, the IKEA Group has been owned by a foundation in the Netherlands with the profits reinvested in the corporation or used for charitable purposes through the IKEA Foundation.

The IKEA Foundation focused initially on architecture and interior design. Over the years, it has become active in addressing the root causes of child labour as well as endeavours with major partners to promote child rights and education.

IKEA continues to be a vibrant, successful and profitable corporation; in 2012 it opened 11 new stores in nine countries, recruited 8,000 new co-workers with significant growth particularly in China, Russia and Poland, but also in the US and Germany.

IKEA shows that alternative ownership models do not conflict with commercial success. Further, it can be argued that the ownership model has been the foundation of its success allowing the management to take decisions for long-term success; getting buy-in from customers, employees and suppliers, because of the trust that people have in a corporation deeply rooted in the structure of global society.

Source: http://www.ikea.com

---

resist. Foundations and charities should have no qualms about requiring that companies they own do no harm; and to go further by encouraging them to play an active role in furthering the objectives of the foundation/charity.

MUTUAL OWNERSHIP

Mutual ownership is where customers are also owners. Examples are when borrowers and lenders come together as mutual Building Societies, or complex corporations like the Cooperative Group in the UK or S-Group in Finland. The management have a responsibility to run the corporation for customers and share profits with the same group of people. It is deeply engrained in the ownership model to run the corporation responsibly. This is markedly different to using pure competition to drive up standards as each corporation seeks to squeeze maximum return for external shareholders. For example, the economies of scale of big distribution centres and maximum automation are attractive from the pure competition model but more nuanced sustainable operations become possible with stakeholder ownership models.

Mutual ownership models that draw customers in as owners build loyalty and lock them in to buying from the corporation as first and primary choice. Typically, examples of mutual ownership have their roots in the historic path when the company was founded or when it was under the control of a single owner with the power to take an enlightened approach. There are numerous examples of mutual companies being brought to the market (Box 14.3) but we do not see listed companies being taken into mutual ownership.

Mutual ownership models have considerable potential because they are a natural fit for the balanced strategy approach championed in this book.

BOX 14.3 DE-MUTUALIZATION OF BUILDING SOCIETIES

Up to the 1980s, the mortgage market in the UK was dominated by mutual building societies. These were owned by their members delivering services to both borrowers and savers. The Newbury Building Society has survived and is an example with approximately £500m in retail savings and £500m in mortgage loans. Building societies were regarded as old-fashioned and rather dull but they were also very transparent and safe. They built up long-term businesses where members joined as savers, saved enough for a deposit on a house to become borrowers and later in life when the loan is paid off become savers again leading into retirement. These organizations built up a cushion of capital as not all the difference between saving and borrowing rates was expended in administrative expenses. This capital cushion was further foundation for the safety and stability of the mutual corporate model. In the 1990s, the financial engineers turned their attention to unlocking this value through floating many building societies to become banks. Members could be persuaded because they were paid (bribed) with cash or shares as this locked-in value was released; management were keen because there were bonuses to be earned through dismantling the old mutual structure. At the time, this was justified on the basis that shareholder ownership would bring greater efficiency.

In the 2000s, one of the largest ex-building societies, Northern Rock, by then a bank, became the biggest banking failure in British history. The management had been running a high-risk lending model based on money from the money-markets. When the global money markets froze, the business model collapsed. Not all ex-building societies have fared so badly but the greed that led to their conversion to banks took a stable brick out of the foundations of the financial system.

In the 2010s, the attractions of safe transparent funding within communities along the lines of building societies are again looking solid. Governments may regret the rush to deregulate that dismantled these bastions of stable finance and introduce legislation to encourage and support the emergence of new mutual societies.

COOPERATIVES

Cooperatives are owned by their staff so each employee has a direct stake in the business. In corporations where staff expertise is the key resource this can be a good model to get the degree of loyalty and retention the corporation needs. Companies can be founded as cooperatives (Box 14.4); or where the founding entrepreneur has retained control, when they come to step down, they can choose to convert their business into a cooperative rather than sell out if they believe in the family of staff they have built up and want to see it thrive and their legacy survive. Management buy-outs (MBO) by a small group of senior staff are common but often personal financial reward is the motive which makes the cooperative model less attractive. However, where senior management are considering an MBO, and deduce that the staff are the key asset, it is worth considering the cooperative model; particularly where this shares the risk with more people and makes the buy-out more likely to attract support from the banks.

BOX 14.4 ZED BOOKS

Zed Books is a successful independent academic publishing company founded in 1977 based in London. It is a workers' cooperative, publishing cutting-edge academic books from an international perspective. All the original founders have left the company but the company they established continues to thrive.

Zed Books is a critical and dynamic publisher, committed to increasing awareness of important international issues and to promoting diversity, alternative voices and progressive social change. We publish on politics, development, gender, the environment and economics for a global audience of students, academics, activist and general readers. Run as a co-operative, we aim to operate in an ethical and environmentally sustainable way.

Source: http://www.zedbooks.co.uk

Managing the Transition to Shared Ownership

Where a model of shared ownership seems to fit the strategy proposed, some thought needs to be given to transitional arrangements. The route from mutual ownership to a listing on the market is well understood but has been a one-way street. It will require some bold trail blazing by management to navigate taking a listed corporation in the other direction into mutual ownership. It would require management to decide it was an option they would like to pursue, to then put together a financing plan that the banks would support and finally persuade current shareholders to accept being bought out. The first such deal would be ground breaking and a game changer in corporate finance but there are no barriers in principle to taking a listed corporation into mutual or cooperative ownership.

CONCLUSION

The key to delivering a viable strategic option is not only to define the business opportunity, and how to exploit it, but also to put together the required package of resources and define an appropriate corporate structure. Doing this within the existing corporate resources is the simplest method provided this does not constrain strategic thinking or close off valuable opportunities. If additional resources are required, it may be necessary to consider an acquisition or joint venture. The idea presented here, that alternative ownership models could have a role in mainstream corporate strategy, seems revolutionary but only because of the dominance of competitive strategic thinking based on growing shareholder value. It will be a huge challenge to take such ideas into the corporate arena where they will be challenged by investors and questioned by management. There is no harm in putting forward a bold alternative ownership model into the evaluation of options; even if it does not survive, it can open the way to innovative new directions taking the corporation out of the hyper-competitive space into operating in collaboration with society and government.

The model of disinterested shareholder, only concerned with short-term financial gain, can be a barrier to good strategy. Strategic thinking that looks closely at changing the ownership profile can open up more effective strategic options but the current owners will have to be persuaded that such innovative strategy is in their interests.

SUMMARY

To make a strategic option viable it is necessary to decide how to gather the package of resources required in a structure capable of delivery. The structure should be appropriate to the corporation, its stakeholders and the nature of the business.

Organic delivery of the strategy through the organization's own set of resources is the simplest and most easily controlled, where the corporation has the know-how, capability and capital.

Acquisition can be a good method for reasons which include:

- To obtain resources and capabilities;
- Vertical integration to secure sources of supply or the route to market;
- To neutralize a potential competitor;

• To harvest synergies and deliver economies of scale.

Joint Ventures (JV) are set up by partnering corporations and can be good corporate vehicles to exploit the SOS (see Chapter 11).

Considering alternative ownership models, such as foundations, mutual corporations and cooperatives is the logical outcome of putting the mantra of shareholder value to one side and should be considered if the circumstances are right and the strategic rationale is strong.

CHAPTER 15

ANALYSIS OF OPTIONS

The selection of strategy requires deep reflection.

The preceding four chapters have taken the strategy process through a sequence of logical analysis generating a number of fully-configured strategic options. While configuring the options, decisions have had to be made to overcome problems and ensure the resulting strategy is internally consistent and workable. The task now is to step back, evaluate and compare the resulting strategic options. This process is about judgement which cannot be tied down to precise criteria. The best that can be achieved is to present the results in a clear and succinct manner to provide the basis for discussion among those who will have to make the decision over the strategy to adopt.

This chapter provides a methodology to compare strategic options leading to a decision support frame-work to support board-level discussion over which option to select for implementation. The evaluation presented here consists of assessing whether each option is 'appropriate', 'feasible' and 'desirable'; and linking this with a financial assessment and an assessment of risk. Finally, the scenarios are brought into play to judge how each strategic option fits with different possible futures. The decision support framework described and explained in this chapter comprises the Evaluation Matrix (Table 15.1) and Scenario Matrix (Table 15.2) which together are the basis for comparing and selecting options.

APPROPRIATE

Is the strategy appropriate to the circumstances the corporation faces?

This is a check that the strategy meshes with the findings of the strategic appraisal, makes appropriate use of corporate capabilities and has worked around any limitations and constraints. An important test to apply is how resilient the strategy is to change in the external environment. Where the strategy has made assumptions about the future, how dependent is success on those assumptions? For example, if the strategy relies on a particular regulatory framework, what are the consequences if it changes? Could the corporation be saddled with capital equipment and facilities that are no longer viable? Where the strategy assumes that a new regulatory framework will be introduced; what are the consequences of delay? Will the corporation have sufficient cash flow to survive in the near-term? Strategies arising from examination of the opportunities of the Sustainable Revolution will be particularly at risk from political posturing as governments juggle electoral concerns with the policy challenges of sustainability. The most resilient strategies will work with, and without, the appropriate regulatory support, perhaps with key approval gateways to commit resources as circumstances dictate.

FEASIBLE

Is it feasible to gather the resources to deliver the strategy?

The key resource will often be the capital required. Has the strategy identified the source of capital or a mechanism to gain access to the capital required? Another aspect of feasibility is whether the corporation has the capabilities required, or whether the strategy is designed to obtain the capabilities required. An issue that might be important is whether government agencies will allow the strategy, or can be persuaded to allow the strategy. Fundamental will be whether shareholders will support (or can be persuaded to support) the strategy. This might depend on whether the strategy is desirable.

DESIRABLE

Will stakeholders find the strategy desirable?

Will the management team of senior executives and managers find the strategy desirable? Responsible management should focus attention on making a judgement of what is good for the long-term success of the corporation. However, it is worth considering whatever personal concerns there might be over career and rewards if only to park such concerns to one side. Senior executives should be expected to provide an impartial analysis. The management are in a very strong position, with full access to information and in-house expertise, to make a judgement about whether the strategy has a good chance of success.

Will the shareholders find the strategy desirable? Where the shareholder register is dominated by short-term investors, their concern will be the short- to medium-term financial return with a view to the likely impact on share price and dividends. However such investors actually have little power and influence, simply selling out if the strategy proposed will not deliver the return they expect. The investors with power and influence are those with significant holdings and intending to remain as shareholders for some time. These will be very interested in the proposed strategy and its long-term impact on the fortunes of the corporation. Long-term investors may have motives that go wider than a financial return and these should be considered in light of the strategy proposed. Care is required, at this low point in the evolution of the corporate landscape, to avoid the blinkered assumption that a corporation has a fiduciary responsibility to maximize the financial return to shareholders. There is a fiduciary duty not to disadvantage minority shareholders but maximizing shareholder value is a concept, not a rule to be obeyed blindly. Assessing the strategy on its impact on shareholder value will come later in the evaluation as a factor to consider but it should not be the prime driving factor.

FINANCIAL EVALUATION

The method of financial evaluation of each strategic option should be consistent. It is also sensible to use a method favoured by the corporate finance team and even better to have the valuation carried out by the corporate finance team working with strategists. Discounted cash flow may be used or other recognized valuation metrics. The detail of the methodology is outside the scope of this book but some general guidance is offered. First, valuations over a short timescale may be more accurate but are less useful; valuations over a longer time frame are more useful but less accurate. This quandary is intrinsic to financial evaluation. The way to handle this dilemma is to view the financial evaluation as guidance rather than fact. Second, the valuation figure means nothing separated from the underlying assumptions used to generate the numbers. The assumptions can be of more strategic interest to decision makers than the headline figure. This means that the financial analysis should have a set of key assumptions as well as a set of numbers.

RISK

The factors that need to be considered to assess risk will depend on the corporation and its business. Financial exposure should always be considered. Where the risk is inherently high but the strategy can run through a series of decision points, before committing to large-scale investment, this could attract a low overall risk score. Another way to keep overall risk within acceptable bounds is if the strategic option is structured to share the risk with other parties.

Table 15.1   Evaluation Matrix

	Option 1	Option 2	Option 3
Appropriate	0–5	0–5	0–5
Feasible	0–5	0–5	0–5
Desirable	0–5	0–5	0–5
AFD score	**0–15**	**0–15**	**0–15**
Financial valuation	£	£	£
Level of risk	L/M/H	L/M/H	L/M/H

Key: L = Low;   M = Medium;   H = High

FUTURE PROOFING

The final input to complete the decision support framework is to consider the strategic options against the scenarios of possible futures completed earlier as a separate activity outside strategy formulation. Crafting the strategic options will have had to consider possible positive and negative changes in the external environment but this is prone to wishful thinking as the strategy architect goes as far as possible to ensure the strategy can succeed. The separation between strategy formulation and scenario generation is important as a check on how each strategic option will fare in different possible futures. The matrix of options against scenarios becomes a useful guide to use in conjunction with the evaluation matrix as illustrated in Table 15.2.

Table 15.2   Scenario Matrix

	Option 1	Option 2	Option 3
Scenario 1	√	–	√
Scenario 2	X	–	√√
Scenario 3	–	√	X

Key: √ √ = Very good fit;   √ = Good fit;   – = Neutral;   X = Poor fit

An option which will work in all scenarios is a safe option; while an option which works only in one scenario would require careful thought as to how it could be implemented safely. Where an option is very attractive in one particular scenario, perhaps delivering a much greater financial return, thought should be given to how to cover the risk that the future will not be the future desired. In the example in

Table 15.2, Strategic Option 3 looks attractive but would struggle in Scenario 3, while Strategic Option 2 would be the safe option. The Scenario Matrix does not drive the decision process but supports discussion over the selection. Although the strategy may include measures to attempt to influence aspects of the future to strategic advantage, the trap to avoid is belief that the corporation has control over the future. The scenarios should not be manipulated to fit the strategy or you could end up with a work of fiction which bears little relation to the real-world. The scenarios should be kept as an independent check and the assessment of the strategic fit made dispassionately.

CONCLUSION

The Evaluation Matrix and Scenario Matrix together comprise the decision support framework for comparing and selecting options. It is not a scoring system where the highest score overall wins but a set of structured information to support wide-ranging discussion. Strategy is not like a project proposal to the board that might get nodded through if the numbers look good; strategy selection can have fundamental long-term consequences. When the strategic options are considered at board-level, a broad-based discussion is likely to follow, over a number of meetings, as the breadth of experience and insight of board members chews over the options. It is unlikely that there will be a straight vote over the options presented; it is more likely that discussion will dig into making changes and consideration of other possibilities such as running two strategies in parallel or cherry picking the best from different strategies. The strategy team should expect to be asked for additional analysis and expect to scope alternatives before a particular strategy emerges as the preferred choice.

SUMMARY

In this chapter, a decision support framework is presented for the comparison of strategic options. The elements of the framework are:

- Is the strategy *appropriate* to the circumstances the corporation faces?
- Is it *feasible* to gather the resources to deliver the strategy?
- Will stakeholders find the strategy *desirable*?
- The *financial analysis* enters the overall evaluation as a guide to value generation locked to a set of key assumptions.
- *Scenarios* are used as an independent check of the strategic fit of the strategy with changes in the external business environment which are outside the corporation's control.

PART IV

DELIVERING THE STRATEGY

A strategy that is filed away is little better than waste paper.

A good strategy based on deep analysis, which has been constructed carefully and is consistent with the macro business context, but seen by only a few people at the top of the organization has little value. To fulfil its potential, strategy has to become live, gaining buy-in from investors, enthusing staff and achieving support from a wide range of stakeholders.

The implementation of strategy, as responsibility rises up the agenda, is both harder and easier than launching conventional strategies. It is harder because of the challenge of driving forward a transformation that goes beyond the confines of the corporation's direct power and control. It is easier because the strategy has been designed through understanding the challenges faced by government and society so that there is likely to be a natural fit with people's expectations and aspirations – when they understand the rationale.

The implementation of strategy will be welcomed by people who understand how it benefits them and can see that it will be a better future but it will also be opposed, not only by vested interests who stand to lose out but also by the natural human reaction to be wary of change; opposition could be for no better reason than 'this is how it has always been done'. Overcoming opposition is about explaining the positive view and giving people who embrace the concept the space to take the strategy forward. There is a need for top-down command and control but successful implementation requires more than prising open closed doors; it is better to use engagement to open doors by oiling hinges and persuading people to turn the handle.

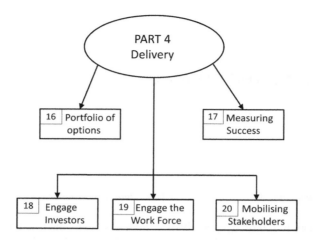

Figure P4.1   Structure Part VI

This part is structured into four chapters. In Chapter 16, the special case of strategy as a portfolio of options is considered because of the high potential this has to help the executive board navigate through the real-world challenges of implementation during periods of disruption and uncertainty. Measuring success is the theme taken up in Chapter 17 leading to the important issues of engaging investors, the work force and other stakeholders (Chapters 18–20).

CHAPTER 16

PORTFOLIO OF OPTIONS

When the external environment is in a state of flux, adaptability becomes more important than perfect adaptation.

The strategy of a corporation should be clear-cut and well defined but there are situations where a single strategy can box the corporation into a corner. This may not matter when the external business environment is in a predictable steady state. Perfect adaptation to a particular niche can maximize profits. However, when the external environment is in a state of flux, and there is uncertainty in areas such as technology, markets and the challenge of shifting to sustainable policy, adaptability becomes more important than perfect adaptation.

A solution to uncertainty is a portfolio of strategic options. This goes further than a portfolio of products and services to embrace a portfolio of different business models. The portfolio approach can be used to balance cash flow within the corporation and can also be used to balance uncertainty. Of particular interest are the additional insights that the challenges of sustainability can bring to the portfolio approach.

BALANCING CASH FLOWS

The growth market share matrix developed by Bruce Henderson of the Boston Consulting Group in the 1970s illustrates how cash generating businesses can complement cash consuming businesses to provide a balanced portfolio of business units. This model is a staple of MBA programmes and a useful way to look at a range of businesses under the corporate umbrella.

Using the BCG Growth-Share Matrix, a company's business units can be classified into four categories based on the combination of market growth and market share. Market growth indicates an attractive industry and relative market share indicates that the business unit has a competitive advantage over its competitors. An assumption underpinning the model is that a growing market requires investment in assets to increase capacity and therefore results in the consumption of cash.

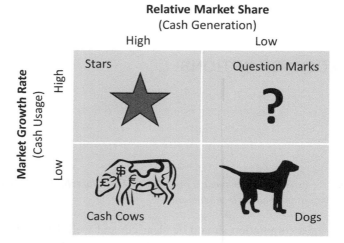

Figure 16.1   The BCG growth-share matrix

Thus the position of a business in the growth-share matrix provides an indication of its cash generation and its cash consumption.

The four categories are:

- *Cash cows*: As leaders in a mature market, cash cows generate cash which can be used to fund the corporation's activities. These may continue to generate cash over many years but it is prudent to expect that these will be superseded at some point as the industry evolves and customers' needs change.
- *Stars*: Stars are operating in high growth markets where they have a high relative market share. If a star can maintain its large market share, it will become in due course a cash cow as the market matures. The portfolio of a diversified company should nurture a number of stars to become the next generation of cash cows.
- *Question marks*: Question marks are operating in high growth markets, consuming large amounts of cash, but because they have a low market share they do not generate much cash. The result is large net cash consumption. A question mark has the potential to gain market share and become a star (and later a cash cow), but if the question mark does not succeed in becoming a market leader, then it may degenerate into a dog when the market growth declines. Management should examine carefully whether investment in question marks is likely to provide a long-term return on investment.
- *Dogs*: Dogs have low market share and a low growth rate and thus neither generate nor consume a large amount of cash. Such businesses trap cash

in businesses with little potential. Such businesses are candidates for divestiture to release cash to invest elsewhere.

Balancing cash flows is an effective way to ensure the corporation has the capital it needs without paying a premium to commercial lenders or bond holders. Setting the balance requires confidence about cash flows which requires assumptions about stability in the macro business environment. Balancing cash flows can become a meaningless exercise if these assumptions do not hold true. Are 'cash cows' grazing in safe pastures or are they 'cash dinosaurs' waiting for the event that wipes them out? Are the 'stars' part of a secure constellation or shooting stars about to come crashing down to earth? Balancing cash flows becomes truly valuable when combined with balancing uncertainty.

BALANCING UNCERTAINTY

It is deeply engrained in sound business practice that a company needs a portfolio of products or services to underpin security of revenue generation. As the current offerings generate turnover, there are new offerings in the pipeline and obsolescent products or services reaching the end of their lives. At the strategic level, a portfolio of businesses (or business units) is required to underpin the continued profitability of the corporation. As the current business units generate turnover, there are new lines of business in the pipeline and obsolescent business models ready to be divested or closed. Technology can make some business models obsolete as Schumpeter's waves of creative destruction ripple through the industry while other business units can be destabilized by shifting consumer behaviour, government policy or the vagaries of an uncertain world.

To balance the uncertainties, the corporation can make a whole series of seed investments in a variety of potential lines of business, operating according to a range of business models. This requires deploying some resources in a speculative manner and can be seen by the accountants as detrimental to short-term profits. Such use of resources can be justified to those wearing financial binoculars as a hedge against an uncertain future.

The management of a portfolio of businesses to survive and exploit uncertainty differs from a financial portfolio approach. Management decisions revolve around not only what the financial spread sheets contain but 'cash cows' need to be monitored for health to ensure they do not keel over unexpectedly, and 'stars' need to be monitored to assess their potential. On one hand, management should reinforce success; on the other, obsolescent cash-generating businesses should be divested while they still have sufficient cash flow to justify a valuation.

Adopting strategy as a portfolio of options requires close analysis of future potential and future risk, to decide: where to make seed investments; when to ramp up investment in these fledgling businesses; and when to withdraw. This can be seen as parallel to management by cash-flow because fledgling businesses need cash and mature businesses generate cash but cash flow is a symptom; it is far more effective to manage by strategic judgement with cash flow management used as a supporting function. Portfolio strategy is more resilient than focussing on one strategy but the approach takes management resources and needs continual monitoring. This approach is particularly useful in the situation where sustainability is judged to be strategically significant.

SUSTAINABILITY VIEW

Strategy defined as a portfolio of options is particular suited to the commercial landscape viewed through the lens of sustainability. Not all boards of corporations will be convinced that sustainability is a prime strategic driver – or not yet – but where sustainability is judged to be strategically significant the portfolio approach can be geared to the fundamental logic of sustainability. The assumption that underpins such an approach is that by force of circumstance sustainability will become the foundation of twenty-first-century economy and society. As alternative policies become ever more damaging and ever more worrying for the general population, leaders across society will be forced to act. There is inevitability about the shift towards more sustainable policy but little certainty about how and when. These are the circumstances that fit perfectly with strategy as a portfolio of options.

There can be no single template for portfolio strategy geared to sustainability as the opportunities are so diverse and their fulfilment will be part of a complex and potentially chaotic transition. A methodology is presented in the chapter 'Profiting from the Transition' in *Adapt and Thrive: The Sustainable Revolution* (McManners 2008): 211–223. This provides a way to structure analysis to assess current lines of business as well as manage a portfolio of nascent new businesses established in response to the opportunities identified. The strength of this particular methodology is that it takes into account the reality of the existing business while charting a route into the future through a period when value destruction will be common (McManners 2008). The wrecking ball will land most heavily on those businesses cemented into the past. Agile businesses that start the transition early will be able to minimize the loss of value and lay new foundations for corporate success to rebuild value in new and innovative ways.

CONCLUSION

Strategy as a portfolio of strategic options is resilient and adaptable but the flexibility and responsiveness comes at the price of suboptimal commercial efficiency. Where a single strategy can be demarcated that maximizes the use of corporate resources mobilized to exploit opportunities, this is likely to deliver the unswerving focus capable of delivering maximum financial return. Where there is uncertainty and the possibility of strategic failure, it becomes vital to hedge risk through actively managing more than one strategic option. Where there is high confidence in the core strategy, the alternative strategic options could be small investments, little more than insurance against the unexpected. Where there is significant doubt about commercial success, management has a dilemma; whether to invest resources to increase resilience, putting short-term profits at risk, or make assumptions to allow a more focussed approach where, if the assumptions are borne out, profits are likely to be higher.

SUMMARY

- When the external environment is in a state of flux, adaptability becomes more important than perfect adaptation.
- The management of a portfolio of businesses can be used to balance cash flow and to balance uncertainty.
- Where sustainability is judged to be strategically significant a portfolio of strategic options can be geared to the essential logic of the transition to a sustainable future.

CHAPTER 17

MEASURING SUCCESS

What gets measured gets managed.

At the operational level, it is a fundamental expectation that management should measure performance against targets. At the strategic level, trying to set targets and measure success is problematic because strategic objectives do not easily translate into specific measurable outcomes. Operational measures, on which middle managers rely, might be contained within the framework of a corporate plan, but strategy is at a higher level. The analogy of a super-tanker illustrates the point. The ship will have a range of systems with gauges and dials showing everything from engine performance and fuel tank levels to outside temperature, wind speed and current heading. A ship's captain sitting on the bridge reading through all these dials is not doing his/her job; that should be delegated to the officer of the watch. The captain needs to know where the ship is meant to be heading and judging when and where the next change of direction is due, scanning the horizon for other ships and possible danger. The task is looking for a particular reference point that indicates that the time is right to change heading, reading the state of the sea and glancing at the charts for underwater obstructions. The ship's operational systems are not brought to the captain's attention except when there is an issue that could affect the progress of the ship. Chief executives need similarly sparse information with strategic targets and measures of success which are sufficient, appropriate and useful to the strategic direction of the corporation.

The aim of this chapter is to focus on generating strategic measures of success which reflect back to the start of the strategic process to confirm whether the corporation is on-track to deliver the agreed strategic objectives. There will be financial and operational targets but strategic targets sit above these to test whether the strategy is working and what may be holding it back.

FOCUS ON STRATEGY

The strategic process has produced a statement of core purpose. This is likely to be too general to measure directly in any meaningful way. It is more likely that objectives a level below this will be more amenable to statements of desirable outcomes. The aim is to identify the pivotal points which determine whether the strategy succeeds. This may extend well beyond the corporation and the activities over which it has direct control. For example, the strategy may involve challenging the industry status quo. A good strategy may even aim to reconfigure the industry in ways that changes the rules of the industry with the corporation at the centre orchestrating the transformation. For example, an automotive company that has decided the future is hydrogen fuel-cell cars would have as a pivotal issue whether progress can be made towards building a hydrogen supply infrastructure. This may not be the corporations' responsibility, nor under the corporation's control, but it could feature as a strategic measure of success. Adopting such a measure would direct senior management towards working with government, industry bodies, complementors, and even competitors, to drive forward with this issue of critical importance.

An industry will have generic critical success factors, which may have been uncovered during the strategic appraisal. These are capabilities required to operate and win business within the confines of current industry norms. It is useful to identify these, but care is needed if progress against these is used as measures of strategic success. Measuring against current industry success factors would imply a level of stability and permanence of the status quo. Many existing industry success factors may remain valid throughout the implementation of the strategy but the measure of strategic success is not how well the corporation is doing now but how well it is shaping its future and whether it is succeeding at carving out a strategic niche which it can dominate.

For each corporation, and each strategy, the pivotal points where senior management should focus attention will be different. A sporting analogy from outside the world of business illustrates the approach (Box 17.1).

SETTING MEASURES /DEFINING TARGETS

The Balanced Scorecard is perhaps the most widely adopted performance management framework (Kaplan and Norton, 1992, 1996 and 2001). This brings together financial and non-financial measures with the content structured to suit the strategy and the business. The process has most value when the measures are carefully selected to match delivery of the strategy rather than working with a standard template. It has been proposed that sustainability can be implemented through inclusion of appropriate targets within the Balanced Scorecard (Epstein and Wisner 2001). This is something that sustainability directors will seek to champion but here the focus is on core strategy and the selection of key strategic measures to incorporate into the reporting framework; it is unlikely that operational sustainability targets will feature.

BOX 17.1 100M SPRINTER – MEASURING PROGRESS

A sprinter's coach drafts a number of measures to monitor progress including:

- Total hours of training per week/month;
- Total distance run per week/month/year;
- Diet including calories consumed;
- Number of hours of sleep;
- Number of rest days;
- Record of training sessions with number of intervals and times achieved;
- Race records of the athlete and potential opponents.

At a quick glance, this might look like a sensible dashboard of training progress. It would be possible to compare the numbers against the training of other competitors to gauge where training could be longer or diet improved particularly in comparison with the athletes who are the greatest threat. Through the lens of strategic thinking this initial list of measures looks less useful. Strategic measures of success should correlate with the core purpose, which in this example might be suitably bold and ambitious: to become world champion.

An appropriate strategic target would be the time taken to run 100m as this is the pivotal point on which the strategy depends for success. Supporting measures could be:

- Aerobic capacity
- Strength
- Agility
- Mental strength

The coach might gather other supporting data but these measures relate directly to progress in delivering the strategic objective. Note that these bear little relationship to the first draft before thinking through the measures that impinge directly on the pivotal points of the strategy. Good coaches do not pile on huge quantities of training (or not only that) but target training to achieve particular carefully selected outcomes on the journey towards the final outcome. These are selected to develop the capability to succeed. All too often athletes have an impressive training log and a long list of races completed, but unless this is part of a strategy with carefully selected milestones they are unlikely to fulfil their potential.

There will be pivotal points around which the strategy will succeed or fail. Identifying that which must be right or must succeed is a good way to tease out potential measurements of strategic success. Such targets are like military objectives which provide a point of focus to keep senior military commanders applying their effort and resources to where they can have the most impact. There will be a plethora of other measures being reported up the chain of command but only presented to top commanders on an exception basis. Business leaders need similarly focussed targets to provide clarity of purpose with operational data being presented to the chief executive only when there could be something critical happening within the machinery of the corporation. Strategy is about looking forward and driving change to navigate the corporation into new waters. Strategic objectives are the way points along the journey and not to be confused with day-to-day operational data.

The starting point in looking for possible measures and candidate targets is to examine the desired corporate strategic footprint set at the start of generating strategic options (Chapter 11). This will be highly specific to the corporation, its circumstances and the strategy. The test of whether a target or measure is useful and appropriate is whether achieving it (or missing it) has strategic significance. Is this something senior management should focus on? Once a target or measure is set, management will work towards achieving it, taking decisions accordingly. Choosing the wrong set of measures could lead management to grub around in a pile of data to little purpose; choosing appropriate strategic measures should allow management to rise above the operational melee to grasp the opportunities the strategy is designed to exploit.

OTHER STRATEGIC MEASURES

In addition to tangible business outcomes there may be intangible factors vital to the success of the strategy. A prime example is corporate culture. An examination of the existing corporate culture may have received little attention during the logical process of the strategic appraisal but when it comes to implementation of the chosen strategy, corporate culture could be vital. Culture may not be part of the strategy but culture can be the catalyst that allows the strategy to work or provide the barrier that blocks it. If the strategy relies on a significant change in corporate culture, the changes required should be included as one of the measures of strategic success. In addition to the nuts and bolts of making the strategy reality, such as structural change and making key investments, there would need to be a programme to facilitate cultural change. In some circumstances this could become the key measure of success. In extreme circumstances, the corporation may have to establish new Business Units were the required culture can be nurtured from the beginning. These would be allowed to expand to prove the concept with staff encouraged to join the new expanding units which will form the backbone of the new corporation. Staff who cannot embrace the change will find themselves in Business Units no longer at the heart of the corporation and in danger of being shut down or sold.

CONCLUSION

The key measures of success are derived from the desired corporate strategic footprint selected early in the analysis. The financial analysis is always important, particularly as a threshold measurement, but measures that are tied directly into strategic objectives carry most weight. Carefully selected supporting measures also have a useful role in increasing resilience and reducing risk. The targets adopted become the targets that senior management aim for. The place to look for potential targets is by examination of the pivotal points on which success depends. What actions or outcomes would ensure the corporation is firmly set on the path envisaged in crafting the new strategic direction? Lucidity of strategic objectives brings with it clarity of action. It is vital that management provide the clear direction required, and the leadership to carry it through, but it should also be accepted that in a changing world it may be that measuring strategic success is a matter of judgement not easily shoehorned inside a measurement framework.

SUMMARY

- Strategic measures of success should focus on the pivotal points which determine whether the strategy succeeds.
- The measure of strategic success is not how well the corporation is doing now but how well it is shaping its future.
- Identifying that which must be right or must succeed is a good way to tease out potential strategic targets.
- Strategic success is, in the end, a matter of judgement.

CHAPTER 18

ENGAGE INVESTORS

Engaging with investors is set to get more complicated.

Investors have considerable ultimate power over the business and the executive management team, so their aims, concerns and interests are important considerations. However, unless the investor is directly involved in the business or has a seat on the board, investors are generally outside the corporation looking in with a much narrower view than the executive team. They rely on the information provided by the business which is expected to give a fair and accurate picture. A key part of finalizing strategy is to bring the investors on board with clear concise information communicated appropriately. In this chapter the important issues of lining up investors behind the strategy will be considered. There are substantial differences depending on the ownership of the business so this chapter is structured around investor engagement in three ownership models: the listed corporation, the private company and the special case of the start-up business.

RESPONSIBILITY TO INVESTORS

The relationship between the executive management team and investors can be tricky where there are divergent aims. This is most evident where the executives manage the company for their own enrichment rather than to deliver value to shareholders. This problem of the principal agent using their power to cream off excessive rewards became rife with examples like WorldCom and Enron. Enron went through a period of apparently spectacular growth in the 1990s with the management rewarded handsomely until the true state of the business was exposed in 2001 leading to the resignation of CEO Jeff Skilling and bankruptcy the same year (Dharan and Bufkins 2008). This was the background to the Sarbanes-Oxley Act of 2002 (U.S. Senate and House of Representatives 2002). This legislation was aimed at protecting investors through improved disclosure of financial information and more controls over corporate governance. The legislation was a response to the perceived problem but legislation will always be a step behind irresponsible executives looking for the next way to line their own pockets. Trying to control through legislation can also have unintended consequences putting too much focus on the financial return to shareholders. Such legislation supports a deeply engrained perception that the prime fiduciary responsibility of the directors of a company is to deliver financial return to shareholders. At a superficial level this seems right but a simple example illustrates the problem of using financial return to shareholders as the objective rather than regarding it as a consequence of managing the business responsibly (see Box 18.1).

BOX 18.1 COFFEE BAR GOVERNANCE

An investor sets up a coffee bar and employs a manager to run it. The first manager has been found to have been overcharging customers siphoning off the money, and is dismissed. The investor tightens the rules to ensure that all the takings are controlled, recorded and reported. A new manager is appointed, who continues with the lucrative arrangement in which customers are routinely overcharged but this time the additional takings are put through the books. The management is behaving in a way that is compatible with the objective to maximize the return to the investor. In this example, this is clearly not right and not responsible behaviour. There is not only the risk that this arrangement will be exposed, affecting reputation and sales, but how can the investor be sure the manager is acting in their best interests when irresponsibility is engrained in the business model. There is always the danger that the manager will spot another way to squeeze more profit and, with the culture established, it will be fair game to try to find a way to retain the benefits for the manager. The second manager is also dismissed when the system attracts the attention of journalists and negative press reports. The third manager is appointed, with the objectives of operating the coffee bar based on integrity, delivering value to customers and listening to customer needs. Over the short-term, the profits booked are lower but it will be obvious to readers with a commercial feel for the situation that this is more likely to succeed.

Professional managers have responsibilities to all the stakeholders of the business and should behave responsibly and with integrity. Astute long-term investors understand this and look for these attributes when deciding where to invest. However not all investors have a long time horizon. There are investors who would rather the management got into cahoots with them to maximize shareholder value over the short-term to the detriment of other stakeholders. Responsible professional management should push back against such narrow expectations. This is very hard to do when corporate finance modules in business schools have sought to put maximizing shareholder value at the centre of the strategic process supported by published guidelines, designed with good intent, but focussed on protecting the financial interests of shareholders.

Responsibility to investors is not something easily controlled by rules and regulations. In fact overbearing rules could have the reverse effect of encouraging anything goes as long as it not prevented by the rules. Responsibility has to be engrained and responsibility to investors cannot be separated from wider responsible behaviour. In a culture in which it is acceptable to ignore other stakeholders to maximize the return to shareholders, it will seem normal for management to squeeze out maximum personal gain allowed by the rules. As the concept of business responsibility is rediscovered, the relationship between investors and management is set to change.

CATEGORIES OF INVESTOR ENGAGEMENT

There are substantial differences between how to engage with investors in a variety of situations. The managers of a listed business have to sell the strategy to equity markets where short-termism is endemic and the expectation is for continuous improvements in the figures year-on-year or quarter-on-quarter. The executive team within a privately owned company have, potentially, much more flexibility but need to persuade the owners to support the strategy. The start-up business is where there is the greatest flexibility and the most potential to set the business on a sustainable path through careful selection of investors. The common thread is that management get the investors they deserve. Responsible management will attract and retain responsible investors to the benefit of both parties.

START-UP BUSINESS

The start-up company has the most freedom as to how to engage with its investors but also the most pressing need to get investors on board to provide the necessary capital. The situation when the business is first established is the only point in the life of the business when there is complete freedom to set the rules. This freedom can be exploited by entrepreneurs to establish the business exactly as they believe it should operate. It is in the nature of entrepreneurs to be quick to spot opportunities and lead the way. When they realise that doing business in the age of responsibility will be different, they will consider new business models which make success more certain and the route to realization of their dreams a smoother ride. Corporations can also consider utilizing new venture business models in innovative ways but convincing corporate shareholders may not be easy.

For the new business, without a corporate sponsor, this is when the management are under pressure to establish the business and a prime consideration is to raise the capital required. In this situation there is a temptation to focus on winning the investment when the real priority is for the executive team to weigh up the potential investors. A strong business plan will attract investors; the challenge is identifying the type of investor you want and persuading them to invest. If the rationale for the business is sound and is pitched to a wide audience there should be a number of interested investors (a dearth of interest from investors is a sign that the proposed strategy is weak and needs to be re-evaluated). Assuming that the strategy is robust, and attracts a number of interested investors, it is important to focus on selecting the investor that is the best fit for the business.

A typical first stage investment is likely to come from a 'business angel' (the term given to high-net-worth individuals who invest in early-stage companies). The term 'Business Angel' describes well the sort of person that is most useful to the business. Of course the investor will want to be sure that the balance of risk to potential return is favourable, but from the company viewpoint this person has to bring added-value such as particular expertise, contacts within the industry or understanding of early-stage company growth. The added-value could be as simple as willingness to invest without interfering and being patient to let the company get established without demanding an early exit.

As the company becomes established and the business plan starts to deliver on its promise, the business becomes attractive to Venture Capitalists (VC). This is where the management need to take great care. A common blunder made by successful early-stage companies, hungry for cash to capitalize on a good business concept, is to accept the advances of a venture capitalist only to discover their influence is entirely focussed on growing a story that will let them sell at a profit in three to five years' time. This is a common VC business model so both sides of the early-stage funding market have to understand and manage the competing objectives. Where an entrepreneur is after making a quick buck, before moving on to other ventures, a conventional VC relationship may work just fine, but the approach championed in this book is that responsible management for the long-term is intrinsically the best approach. VCs will have to up their game as more entrepreneurs see the logic in building sustainable businesses. There are VCs that see this change coming and are starting to change their focus but there is an inherent incompatibility between the VC concept of squeezing a company for maximum uplift in short-term value and investing for long-term success. It is the responsibility of management to be selective with the potential investors they are willing to engage with and careful in signing away ownership.

The VC route might be the only way to gain access to investment capital in the quantity required and, on the positive side a good VC can be useful. A responsible VC will do more than grow the investment story for a quick sale and work towards supporting the establishment of a sustainable business with long-term potential. Of course savvy responsible investors can work out whether the business has a long-term future, so responsible investors and responsible VCs will tend to migrate towards each other. This is a positive sum game of working responsibly together matching good businesses with solid investors. There are signs that investors are beginning to understand the potential of responsible investing but VCs have such deeply ingrained business processes that change for them may be slow in coming. Unfortunately in the current corporate world the term 'responsible VC' is almost an oxymoron. Until the VC community adopt the concepts of responsible business, entrepreneurs should be very careful with the selection of a VC and examine critically what they can offer in addition to the cash.

The start-up business is not just the realm of the entrepreneur but established corporations can benefit from launching new ventures controlled at arms-length. In some cases the corporation may have only a minority stake, or no formal ownership role at all, but it will take some time for such ground-breaking concepts to become acceptable. This situation can arise where the corporation sees its future as orchestrating a loose network of cooperating businesses working to mutual advantage. A specific example is where, during strategy formulation, the potential of a stakeholder ownership model may have been identified. For the existing corporation, changing the ownership model may be a step too far but establishing a new entity could be relatively easier. This is provided the owners of the parent corporation can be persuaded of the benefits and allow the management to proceed without vetoing such action.

In summary, at the point of formation there is considerable freedom to set the business on a particular path. Management should use this power responsibly to set the business on a sustainable path fully compatible with current challenges and opportunities. This will require pushing back against irresponsible investors wanting to use the business as a vehicle to make short-term financial gain. The key to engaging with investors for a start-up business, before investors are locked in, is to select carefully which investors are allowed on board.

THE PRIVATE COMPANY

The owners of a private company have discretion over the strategy they want the business to pursue. This could be anywhere in the range from supporting altruistic intentions to squeezing maximum cash out of the business without concern for the consequences. The owner(s) have considerable freedom and flexibility but the executive team have only the scope for action that the owner will authorize. In this situation, the management have to persuade the owner to support the proposed strategy.

The historic path that the business has followed may be significant. An obvious example is where the business is the commercial arm of a charity so expected to have responsibility hard-wired into the organization. The business is more than an investment but also an integral part of the delivery of the charity's objectives. At the other end of the spectrum, the business may have been bought by investors specializing in private equity so that the management team have very limited opportunity other than to squeeze the business for maximum short-term return. Another example is a family-owned business which may have established a loyal workforce within the wider family of the business. Provided the family have the executive roles they desire, and a dividend that satisfies their needs, authorization for a strategy that takes into account a wide range of stakeholders may be easy to obtain. For a business still owned by its founder, the character and intention of this person can have huge influence over culture and strategy. It is interesting that a number of entrepreneurs take their business down the conventional route leading to a listing on the equity markets only to use their new-found wealth to set up a charitable foundation working with issues about which they are passionate. Another route to a similar destination is to retain ownership of the business but to set a direction which can deliver the outcomes in society that the entrepreneur wants to support. This unconventional route can be hard if the business employs executives indoctrinated by the leading MBA programmes. This situation will start to reverse as society starts to expect more of business, and business leaders spot the opportunities but, as is always the case, the syllabus in business schools will lag behind the emerging reality.

In summary, proposing a strategic direction to the owners of a private company, the executive team have to navigate the duality of total freedom to put forward bold and responsible strategy together with the constraint of accepting the owner's decision. The focus of investor engagement is *persuasion*.

LISTED CORPORATION

The corporate world is dominated by listed companies so engagement with the equity markets is a common challenge. Many investors in listed shares are faceless and fickle, switching ownership regularly and often taking a short-term view. The relationship between the investors and executive managers is like competing in a three-legged race. The common leg that ties them together is the delivery of consistent short-term results. This is what the market expects and what the management are required to deliver. This hobbles the business making it more difficult to deliver long-term objectives. It would be better to release the management team (and investors) from this artificial constraint to provide space to run the real business in a responsible manner. When management are freed from worrying about short-term market sentiment they are empowered to do what is right for the business over the longer-term. The investors that buy into the strategy will stay aboard but the short-term investors may sell and move on. The share price is likely to take a dive, but other savvy investors looking for real value may see it as a buying opportunity.

It is suggested here that the prime objective of engaging with the equity markets is to attract investors with long time horizons. Corporations with a number of stable investors on the share register can develop a relationship with particular fund managers and large investors to discuss strategic intentions and win some respite from market short-termism. It happens all too often that management are given incentives for short-term share price growth leading to suboptimal strategy through the period of tenure of a series of CEOs each lasting two or three years as they focus on attempting to reach their targets before departing. Responsible management should resist joining this merry-go-round and manage for sustainability, resilience and real business success.

The management of listed corporations are always under the critical eye of the markets. Care must be taken to report accurately and it should be expected that many analysts will focus on the short-term results. Despite this, management should have the confidence to put forward and defend strategy for a successful sustainable business.

In summary, the focus of engaging with the equity markets is to *sell* the strategy, particularly to the large fund managers that tend to buy and hold without bending the strategy to satisfy the short-term demands of high frequency traders.

THE EMERGING INVESTOR MARKET

Engaging with investors is set to get more complicated, and more thought-provoking, as support grows for sustainable business working on behalf of all its stakeholders. The point of company formation is particularly stimulating when there is complete freedom to define the objectives of the new venture and set rules through a shareholder agreement. If these objectives stray into a role that is semi-charitable many investors will be put off. However there is space at this point in the corporation's life to set higher objectives than pure profit and attract investors with other objectives than pure profit such as ethical investors, ethical investment funds and even investment funds held by charitable organizations. The idea that charities should invest their funds for maximum return without looking closely at the nature of the investments is obsolescent. The stage beyond this is when charities actively manage their investments to support the delivery of their charitable objectives accepting the possibility of a lower return as a consequence. This seems like unorthodox investing according to current norms but these changes are likely to be adopted by many big investors (such as pension funds, local authorities and high-net-worth individuals) because the overall impact of better investing is stable, profitable corporations working in tune with society. Investors get security and a solid return; companies get the freedom to plan for long-term success.

SUMMARY

- We are entering an age when investor dynamics will favour sustainable business.
- Investor engagement will change as the advantages of responsible business permeates both the management and investor communities. Responsible management will attract responsible investors in a win-win alliance.
- Executives have a professional responsibility to be effective stewards of the business for the long-term and for all stakeholders. This may mean pushing back against the demands of speculators and investors with a short time horizon.
- Entrepreneurs should *select* which investors they invite on board and be particularly wary of VCs operating to the old model of venture capital.
- The managers of private companies have considerable freedom to pitch novel business strategy through a process of *persuasion*.
- Executives in listed corporations should *sell* sustainable, long-term strategy to the equity markets with the aim of building a stable investor community.

CHAPTER 19

ENGAGE THE WORKFORCE

Respect breeds respect.

The corporation exists because of the sum total of the efforts of its past and present employees; its future is the sum total of the efforts of the employees going forward. Engaging with the work force is therefore crucial to taking the corporation in a new strategic direction. Transforming the corporation will not happen unless the employees make it happen. A good strategy is at risk of failure if the work force opposes it; whilst a strategy with weaknesses can be bolstered to become an effective strategy if the work force engages in shaping and improving it. Employees should be drawn inside the process to share ownership of the strategy and encouraged to influence the detail of implementation. Persuading the work-force to buy-in to the strategy is a very powerful way to ensure successful delivery. This process cannot wait until implementation; employee engagement should begin from the strategic appraisal; ramp up when launching the strategy and continue as the new strategic direction is bedded in. This is the essence of effective organizational Change Management, where the culture and values of the organization are explicitly recognized and managed as part of any change, through communication, measurement systems, job design, processes, training and other 'levers'.

The aim of this chapter is to discuss aspects of employee engagement in so far as it directly affects the process of changing the strategic direction of the corporation.

PRE-ENGAGEMENT

The initial strategic appraisal may have identified strategic work-force issues to take into account when crafting the strategy. In which case, how these have been incorporated needs to be communicated. In addition, the process will certainly have involved a number of employees, both directly and indirectly. Therefore, it has to be assumed that some aspects of the strategic analysis have entered the corporations' grapevine. It is human nature for the work force to be extremely interested in the strategic analysis, and particularly in conclusions which could have significant impact on job roles and employment. Before the strategy is announced, there is the risk of rumours circulating making people concerned for their future. To reduce this risk, management should draw input from across the corporation as the strategy is being considered – and are seen to do so. There is a need for commercial confidentiality as the strategic options are debated but this should be balanced with sufficient openness to reassure the work force that their input in valued. Seeking opinion and allowing staff to input their views will make the process seem much more transparent even though the findings are likely to remain confidential until key decisions have been taken at board level.

STRATEGY LAUNCH

When the board have decided upon the strategy, it should be communicated first to the key people within the corporate family who will be taking the strategy forward. They should be briefed in sufficient detail to understand the key elements of the strategy, why the strategy is needed and the outline plan for the implementation. These people need, not only reassurance that their future is locked into the corporation's future but also confidence that the future will be with a corporation that knows where it is going. This message should include how the business delivers value to society to mobilize a level of buy-in that goes deeper than the loyalty of securing the next month's salary.

In the circumstance where there is bad news to communicate, such as job losses or plant closures, these should be communicated without delay with all the bad news timed together. If bad news is allowed to trickle out piecemeal, people cannot be certain that there may be further bad news just over the horizon which affects them. Where there are to be closures or job losses everyone affected should be given the opportunity to apply for other jobs within the corporation – where possible. For those for whom there is no place in the future corporation there should be support and assistance. The aim should be to get the bad news out of the way in a way that does not sour the launch of the new strategy or distract from the prime task of rebuilding the corporate family around the new strategy.

It can be a very unsettling time when a new strategy is launched. Resistance should be expected but the long-term good of the corporation should come before the current work force defending their position. Those who oppose the new direction, and are unwilling to embrace the changes, should expect to be eased out. Responsible management should deal fairly and firmly with redundancy, where this is required, so that the air can be cleared as soon as possible to move forward with the new corporate direction.

EMBEDDING STRATEGY

Following the immediate action to launch the strategy, management should move on to embed the strategy and steer the corporation in the new direction. This will require staff engagement at all levels to communicate the strategy, explain the rationale and identify levers that can be used to effect change. This is a further chance to listen to comments, and complaints, as well as encourage people to put forward suggestions for improvements. Where suggestions from staff are adopted and implemented, the benefits go beyond the specific advantages of the adjustment made, showing that the corporation is listening and values its work force.

Through this period of change, management should treat the employees as valued stakeholders. By dealing openly and fairly with staff it should be expected that staff respond by working to make the strategy work, overcoming problems and seeking solutions for issues which have not been anticipated or where plans are weak or incomplete and need improving. Whatever culture the corporation has had in the past, it is suggested that the most effective culture to fit the era of responsible business is one of cooperation between managers and staff, an attribute sometimes lacking in the aggressive corporate cultures spawned from a business environment dominated by competition. This is a two-way street with plain talking to face down irrational and unreasonable demands from workers just as much as listening and responding to the worker's concerns as part of a robust and effective partnership.

The most successful corporations will already have a cooperative culture where people are able and willing to work together towards share objectives. In this case, implementation should be relatively easier, once the elements of the new strategy have been explained. In other cases, the culture may hinder change as people fight turf wars and defend the status quo. Using the strategic process to overcome such cultural weakness is valuable in itself to lift the corporation out of its stupor and increase the resilience of the corporation to respond to future challenges.

CONCLUSION

The members of the work force are key stakeholders with strategic value and should be treated with respect. They have the power to damage the corporation and undermine the strategy but they are also in the position to make the strategy work. It is human nature to oppose change and if strategy is imposed without effective employee engagement it can be expected that employee power will be directed towards negative outcomes. Through effective employee engagement, the energies of staff can be directed towards improving the strategy and mobilizing enthusiastic support through sharing a vision of a better, more effective, corporation.

SUMMARY

- Management should draw input from across the corporation as the strategy is being considered.
- When the board have decided upon the strategy, communicating early with the key people who will be taking the strategy forward is vital to a successful launch.
- In the circumstance where there is bad news to communicate, such as job losses or plant closures, these should be communicated without delay.
- To embed the strategy will require staff engagement at all levels to communicate the strategy and explain the rationale.

CHAPTER 20

MOBILIZE OTHER STAKEHOLDERS

Building long-term commercial advantage requires mobilizing broad stakeholder support.

Stakeholder concerns have been taken into account throughout the strategic analysis as an integral component of a responsible business approach. Engaging investors and the workforce have been covered in the preceding chapters; in this chapter the strategic issues pertinent to a number of other stakeholders are outlined. Government is the most powerful and important stakeholder so it is important to find alignment with governmental goals. NGOs have little direct power but their ability to influence has grown over the same period that society's trust in business has diminished. The cultivation of links with particular NGOs can be useful where a shared agenda can be found. Finally, the relationship with other corporations is naturally one of rivalry but through a stakeholder perspective it becomes possible to think in terms of positioning the corporation in a stable business ecosystem thus reducing the intensity of rivalry. First, let us consider customers, who are fundamental to the corporation, the strategy and its delivery.

CUSTOMERS

Customer needs are fundamental to each stage of the strategic process because without customers the corporation cannot survive. As the strategic process moves into delivery of the strategy, the marketing function can be expected to take up the running with regard to customer engagement. Marketing input may have played a part in the strategic analysis but when the strategy has been agreed care is needed to align the marketing plan with the chosen strategy. At the strategic level, consideration will have been given to drawing customers close to the corporation, possibly through the ownership structure and certainly through responding to their needs and concerns. To exploit this, it is useful to clarify what it is about the strategy that will help to retain existing customers, recruit new customers and engage with people who might become customers in the future. The strategy team should work with the marketing executives to agree the basis of a consistent approach across the strategy/marketing interface. Where sustainability is a foundation of the strategy, the marketing function should comply with one of the 'commandments' of effective communication: 'Integrate sustainability into your core business and determine your direction before starting to communicate.' (Conrad and Thompson 2013: 299).

GOVERNMENT

Government has wide responsibilities and considerable power through enacting legislation and setting policy. It is therefore important to get on the right side of government. Fortunately the approach presented in this book has brought the concerns and challenges of government inside the strategic appraisal. It has been noted that government can be hamstrung by political restraints so can find it hard to get things done. This is where business can help government – and help itself – by aligning strategy with government imperatives. The question to consider, now that strategy has been formulated is, what can the government do to support the strategy? This seems an odd question in the current business climate of confrontation between business and government, but as business becomes more responsible and mutual trust grows this will become an entirely reasonable question. At its most basic level all that might be required of government is to get out of the way; but there are other issues to consider such as the current regulatory framework, government support programmes and future challenges:

Regulatory Framework

Every industry is subject to a raft of legislation to comply with to be allowed to operate. However, regulation tends to expand to match the size of the perceived problem; reducing the severity of the problem can reduce the need for the regulation. As business improves its credentials for responsibility a bonfire of red tape could be the reward. Although this is unlikely to gather pace before business adopts wholesale change of attitude and culture. Meanwhile, the corporation should determine which regulations may hinder the strategy and prepare a case for change. The case should be couched in terms of the benefits to society, of course, but written with the motive to facilitate the corporate strategy. Accusations of underhand dealing are possible but are unlikely to stick where the ethos of this book has been followed such that the corporate strategy is aligned with society's needs. Responsible business should feel free to campaign for regulatory change wherever and whenever red tape is slowing progress.

Support

Governments attempt to help and encourage the industries that it believes the country needs with incentives and support programmes. Government may not have a great track record of picking winners but it makes sense to work with the intentions of government, to find out what is available and find ways to use such schemes to commercial advantage. The support programmes exist with the aim of building vibrant and successful businesses so corporations should use the schemes to do just that. It should be investigated whether there are technology catapults or regional aid grants available and, if so, to consider bending the strategy to meet the funding requirements. As the corporate strategy has been developed with the needs of government and society in mind, it is likely that government incentives will be found that align with the strategy and can be exploited. There may not be a close match with the stated parameters because deep strategic thinking by the corporation may be ahead of the advice coming from government officials. The corporation should feel free to push the corporate agenda in bidding for support as this might help to move government forward faster, to deliver their aspirations in parallel with corporate objectives.

Future Challenges

Beyond the current regulatory framework and current support packages there is always a fluid debate running about the future. This is too ephemeral for specific strategic plans but engaging in the debate – in forums, studies and consultations – is useful to assist with laying the foundations for future strategy. There can be good opportunities to explore possible new strategic directions. Where the corporation can use the debate to take a lead in the industry this can sow seeds of longer term strategic success. It might be possible to become known and recognized as a case study for the industry to follow. In the UK, the retailer Marks and Spencer has earned good media coverage for its attempt to make its operations more sustainable under its 'Plan A' programme. In the United States, Wal-Mart has been reported on favourably for using its buying power to make its supply chain more sustainable. These sustainability initiatives were limited in scope at first and may not have taken them far along the road to true sustainability but they have been doing more than others in their industry and that has been sufficient to win plaudits and wear the badge of industry leader. Engaging, and being seen to engage, in the future challenges faced by society and government is a valuable opportunity to influence how government policy evolves and keep corporate strategic thinking fresh and up-to-date.

NON-GOVERNMENTAL ORGANIZATIONS (NGOS)

NGOs have become increasingly critical of business, particularly as the standing of some businesses in the community has faltered through pursuing a narrow profit-focus agenda. The role of trusted observer, looking on from the moral high ground, has become influential. This means that where a well-known NGO can be persuaded to support the corporation this can be a valuable vote of confidence. The issue that might steer a NGO towards interest in a particular corporation is typically a potential problem identified somewhere in the corporation's operations exposing the corporation to the threat of negative publicity. A knee-jerk approach could be to identify which NGOs are most likely to cause the corporation problems and work out how to counter. A more enlightened approach is to seek out NGOs who could be enthused by the corporation's new strategic direction because there are potential synergies between the aims and objectives of the NGO and the corporation. Building a relationship with one or more NGOs and earning their support and approval can be valuable but will have to include responding to NGO concerns in a substantive manner to fulfil the corporation's side of the bargain.

OTHER CORPORATIONS

The relationship with other corporations is by default one of rivalry, but stable successful industries have a healthy balance between competition and cooperation. Considering the strategy through the eyes of rival corporations as potential stakeholders can open up perspectives of increased cooperation in ways beneficial to both parties. Industry forums and industry organizations are useful ways to keep up-to-date with industry thinking and to seek ways to influence changes in the industry to suit the corporation's view of the future. This applies particularly to the Shared Operating Space (SOS) (see Chapter 11) where the agenda of cooperation dominates the strategic dialogue. Will the corporation's strategy reshape the industry? Are there industry-wide changes that are vital to strategic success? Which other corporations are vital to facilitating the required changes? Particular issues arise for complementors, suppliers and competitors:

Complementors

Corporations that provide a product or service that sits alongside the corporation's offering will be wary of the launch of a new strategic direction worried that it might impinge on their operating space. The strategy may include a deliberate intention to integrate horizontally, in which case moves could be made to acquire complementors or to think through the consequences of starting to compete against them. If there is no such strategic plan, complementors need reassurance that their commercial position remains sound with discussion about how to enhance the overall customer package to the benefit of both corporations.

Suppliers

The corporations' suppliers will be concerned at a new strategic direction until they understand how it affects them. Where the strategy includes vertical integration, they are right to be concerned, as the corporation seeks to acquire suppliers or invest in the capabilities required to bring upstream activities in-house. Where there is no intention to take over the supply chain, thought should be given to the message to communicate to suppliers. This is likely to include any adjustments which may be required to mesh with the corporation's new strategy. Where this requires investment, the suppliers need to know that their position has a degree of security. For example, a strategic decision may have been made to require higher standards of sustainability from suppliers to allow the corporation take a leadership role within the industry to drive forward changes which can be exploited. This should not be a box-ticking approach but part of a strong commercial strategy to carve out a space for the corporation in a transformed industry.

Competitors

It may seem exceedingly odd to regard competitors as stakeholders in the new strategic direction, but it is worth thinking through the consequences from their viewpoint. They will of course want to defend their UCS and, given the chance, may want to encroach on the corporation's UCS. It may be possible to neutralize this potentially destructive competitive tension by steering competitors to succeed in the SOS, agreeing to cooperate in some areas and specialize in others. If the new strategy is a bold departure from the status quo there may be good opportunities for all parties through investing in new capabilities which makes the old industry rules obsolete. Corporations that stick doggedly to fighting their space may be side-lined as the industry moves forward without them. A strong strategic position is leading the pack driving change but allowing competitors the space to operate without initiating competition based on price.

CONCLUSION

Considering the viewpoint of a range of stakeholders in implementing a new strategic direction may be fruitful depending on the industry and the circumstances encountered. Where strategy has been developed on the basis of exploiting immediate short-term commercial advantage, there is little point in investing time in understanding other stakeholder perspectives. However, where the strategic aim is to build long-term commercial advantage by embedding the corporation firmly in the wider economy, it becomes very important to mobilize stakeholder support. This will include customers, of course, but also government, NGOs and other businesses who can be persuaded to accept that the corporation is unassailable in the niche it has chosen to dominate, and that working alongside would be easier than competing head-to-head.

SUMMARY

- Stakeholder concerns should be taken into account throughout the strategic process including moving towards implementation.
- The strategic engagement with customers requires a consistent approach across the strategy/marketing interface.
- It is important to get on the right side of government to influence regulation, exploit government incentives and join the debate over future challenges.
- Building a relationship with one or more NGOs and earning their support can be a valuable vote of confidence.
- Considering the strategy through the eyes of rival corporations as potential stakeholders can open up perspectives of increased cooperation in ways beneficial to both parties.

CONCLUSION

Business has always been a strong force in the economy and has huge influence in society. Corporations have become adept at persuading people how they should live their lives to grow the market for the corporation's products and services. This apparently successful focus on consumer capitalism is leading the world into an uncertain future of resource limits and environmental degradation. The world needs the power and capability of business more than ever, but with renewed vigour and a clearer focus.

Business's ability to respond is hampered by government regulation and investor's myopic focus on profits. Government will not ease regulations unless business can demonstrate it can be trusted; and business cannot rebuild trust unless it chooses a path where profits are a consequence of doing the 'right' things rather than a single-minded focus on short-term financial return. The core problem is that business has become disconnected from its proper role in society. It is understood that business must make a profit, but operating the corporation to maximize financial return is dismantling the structure of society piece by piece. This is a strong statement and not a fair reflection on all businesses, but where each corporate decision is based on the expected financial return, it perpetuates the idea of business as a money making machine, and it is this idea which is so damaging. As all corporations do the same, only governments are left trying to set policy for the good of society – and it seems to be beyond the capability of current governments around the world to deliver on so many overlapping challenges. The money-making-machine mentality is removing business from a responsible role in society, building up a reservoir of distrust and wrapping business in a straitjacket of regulation.

The twenty-first century corporate challenge is to reconnect business with society, make regulation less necessary and set business free to serve society. This is not the now discredited mantra of de-regulation but the concept of reintroducing responsibility into the DNA of the corporation. This book has laid out a strategic process that sits uneasily with the model of capitalism which is widely championed in the business literature. For those people reading this book with long careers in successful corporations, who have not bent to the fads that ripple through the world of consultancy and businesses schools, this approach may seem little more than common sense; and refreshingly different to the ideas indoctrinated into MBA graduates over the last two decades. Resurgence is needed in commercial realism and common sense to push back against the incestuous drive to increase shareholder value. Corporations can look forward with renewed confidence to a period in which they rebuild trust, find that working with government is fruitful, increase the resilience of the corporation and bolster the cohesion of its family of workers and stakeholders.

Governments are finding it very difficult to broker and implement solutions to the challenges of this age. Business is uniquely capable of acting, where governments cannot; opening up huge opportunities for business to show through strong leadership and its actions that business can be trusted and make the case that business should be given the license to operate at the heart of society in a true partnership with government and civic society.

Business strategy should not be about turning a quick buck through using smoke and mirrors to sell whatever the market will accept to whoever is willing to buy. Strategy should be about clear-eyed observation and logical analysis of the commercial opportunities to support society in the challenges it faces. The businesses that dominate the twenty-first century will focus on serving people's real needs in sustainable ways that do not undermine the future of society living on a finite planet.

REFERENCES

Ansoff, I. 1957. Strategies for Diversification, *Harvard Business Review*, Vol. 35, Issue 5, Sep-Oct 1957: 113–24.

Ballinger, J. 1992. 'The new free-trade heel', *Harper's Magazine*, August 1992.

Barford, V. and Holt, G. 2013. 'Google, Amazon, Starbucks: The rise of 'tax shaming'', *BBC News Magazine* [http://www.bbc.co.uk/news/magazine-20560359; accessed 5 Jan 2014].

BBC 2012. Samsung overtakes Nokia in mobile phone shipments, BBC News, 27 April 2012 [http://www.bbc.co.uk/news/business-17865117; accessed 3 Dec 2013].

BBC 2013a. 'Nokia Microsoft mobile deal gets shareholder go ahead', BBC News, 19 Nov 2013 [http://www.bbc.co.uk/news/business-25005698; accessed 3 Dec 2013].

BBC 2013b. 'Dhaka building collapse: Factories and buyers', 10 May 2013, BBC News Asia [http://www.bbc.co.uk/news/world-asia-22474601; accessed 5 Dec 2013].

Bergin, T. 2012. 'Special Report: How Starbucks avoids UK taxes', Reuters London, 15 Oct 2012 [http://uk.reuters.com/article/2012/10/15/us-britain-starbucks-tax-idUSBRE89E0EX20121015; accessed 6 Jan 2014].

Birch, S. 2012. 'How activism forced Nike to change its ethical game', The Guardian Green Living Blog [http://www.theguardian.com/environment/green-living-blog/2012/jul/06/activism-nike; accessed 23 Nov 2013].

Blackstone 2011. Response to misleading UK news story about former portfolio company Southern Cross, Blackstone Blog, 2 Jun 2011 [http://www.blackstone.com/news-views/blackstone-blog/response-to-misleading-uk-news-story-about-former-portfolio-company-southern-cross; accessed 10 Nov 2013 and URL checked 26 Mar 2014].

Campbell, D., Stonehouse, G. and Houston, B. 2002. 2nd edition (1st edition 1999) *Business Strategy: An Introduction*, Oxford: Butterworth-Heinemann.

Competition Commission 2011. 'Payment Protection Insurance Market Investigation Order 2011', London: Competition Commission.

Conrad, C. and Thompson, M.E. 2013. *The New Brand Spirit: How communicating sustainability builds brands, reputations and profits*, Farnham (UK): Gower.

Cowling, K. and Tomlinson, P.R. 2011. 'Post the 'Washington Consensus': economic governance and industrial strategies for the twenty-first century', *Cambridge Journal of Economics* 2011, 35, 831–52.

Dannenberg, A., Frumkin, H. and Jackson, R. (eds) 2011. *Making Healthy Places: Designing and Building for Health, Well-being, and Sustainability*, Washington: Island Press.

Department for Transport 2011. 'Realising the Potential of GB Rail: Final Independent Report of the Rail Value for Money Study', May 2011 [http://www.dft.gov.uk/rail-value-for-money; accessed 4 Dec 2013].

Dharan, B.G. and Bufkins, W.R. 2008. Red Flags in Enron's Reporting of Revenues and Key Financial Measures, *Social Science Research Network*, (23 July 2008) [http://ssrn.com/abstract=1172222; accessed 6 Jan 2014].

Drucker, P.F. 2007. *The Practice of Management*, Classic Drucker Collection edition (1st edition 1955), Oxford: Elsevier.

Epstein, M.J. and Wisner, P.S. 2001. Using a Balanced Scorecard to Implement Sustainability, *Environmental Quality Management*, Vol. 11, Issue 2: 1–10.

EWEA 2013. 'Wind in power 2012 European statistics,' report dated Feb 2013 [http://www.ewea.org/fileadmin/files/library/publications/statistics/Wind_in_power_annual_statistics_2012.pdf; accessed 16 Nov 2013].

Fisher, D. 2011. 'Japan Disaster Shakes Up Supply-Chain Strategies', Harvard Business School Working Knowledge paper, 31 May 2011 [http://hbswk.hbs.edu/pdf/item/6684.pdf; accessed 5 Dec 2013].

Fisheries Research Services, 2004. Case Study – Brent Spar [http://www.scotland.gov.uk/Uploads/Documents/AE07Brent2004.pdf].

Guerrera, F. 2009. 'Welch condemns share price focus', *Financial Times*, 12 March 2009, New York: Financial Times [http://www.ft.com; accessed 21 Dec 2013].

House of Commons, 2012. Public Accounts Committee: Oral Evidence taken before the Public Accounts Committee on Monday, 12 November 2012, [http://www.publications.parliament.uk/pa/cm201213/cmselect/cmpubacc/716/121112.htm].

House of Lords, 2013. 'Tackling corporate tax avoidance in a global economy: is a new approach needed?' Select Committee on Economic Affairs: 1st Report of Session 2013–14, [http://www.publications.parliament.uk/pa/ld201314/ldselect/ldeconaf/48/48.pdf; accessed 6 Jan 2014].

Insley, J. 2013. Can ethical investing be profitable? *The Telegraph*, 26 March 2013. [http://www.telegraph.co.uk/finance/personalfinance/investing/isas/9952092/Can-ethical-investing-be-profitable.html; accessed 6 Jan 2014].

IPCC, 2013. 'Summary for Policymakers', in *Climate Change 2013: The Physical Science Basis. Contribution of Working Group I to the Fifth Assessment Report of the Intergovernmental Panel on Climate Change*, Stocker, T.F., D. Qin, G.-K. Plattner, M. Tignor, S.K. Allen, J. Boschung, A. Nauels, Y. Xia, V. Bex and P.M. Midgley (eds). Cambridge, United Kingdom and New York, NY, USA: Cambridge University Press.

Jensen, M.C. and Meckling, W.H. 1976. Theory of the frim: Managerial Behavior, Agency Costs and Ownership Structure, *Journal of Financial Economics*, 3(4): 305–60.

John Lewis Partnership 2013. 'Our strategy' [http://www.johnlewispartnership.co.uk/about/our-strategy.html; accessed 6 Dec 2013].

Joshi, R.M. (2009) *International Business*, New York: Oxford University Press.

Kaplan, R.S. and Norton, D.P. 1992. 'The Balanced Scorecard – Measures that Drive Performance', *Harvard Business Review*, Jan-Feb. 1992: 71–79.

Kaplan, R.S. and Norton, D.P. 1996. *The Balanced Scorecard: Translating Strategy into Action*, Boston: Harvard Business School Press.

Kaplan, R.S. and Norton, D.P. 2001. *The Strategy Focused Organization*, Boston: Harvard Business School Press.

Kim, W.C. and Mauborgne, R. 2004. 'Blue Ocean Strategy', *Harvard Business Review*, Oct 2004: 76–84.

Kim, W.C. and Mauborgne, R. 2005. *Blue Ocean Strategy: How To Create Uncontested Market Space And Make The Competition Irrelevant*, Boston: Harvard Business School Publishing.

Lewis, J.S. 1957. Talking to the BBC about his vision for the Partnership, recorded on 15 April 1957.

London Energy Partnership 2007. 'Making ESCOs Work: Guidance and Advice', London: London Energy Partnership. [http://www.lep.org.uk/uploads/lep_making_escos_work.pdf; accessed 24 Nov 2013].

Lowenstein, R. 2004. *Origins of the Crash: The Great Bubble and Its Undoing*, New York: The Penguin Press.

Martenson, C. 2011. *The Crash Course: The Unsustainable Future of Our Economy, Energy, and Environment*, Hoboken (New Jersey): John Wiley & Sons.

Martin, R.L. 2011. *Fixing the Game*, Boston: Harvard Business Review Press.

McDonough, W. and Braungart, M. 2002. *Cradle-to-Cradle: Remaking the Way We Make Things*, New York: North Point Press.

McDonough, W. and Braungart, M. 2013. *The Upcycle: Beyond Sustainability—Designing for Abundance*, New York: North Point Press.

McManners, P.J. 2007. *Cities for People: Removing Cars from Urban Life*. Paper presented at the World Institute for Development Economics Research of the United Nations University (UNU-WIDER) project workshop, Beyond the Tipping Point: Development in an Urban World, London School of Economics and Political Science, 19–20 October 2007.

McManners, P.J. 2008. *Adapt and Thrive: The Sustainable Revolution*. UK: Susta Press.

McManners, P.J. 2009. *Victim of Success: Civilization at Risk*. UK: Susta Press.

McManners, P.J. 2010. *Green Outcomes in the Real World: Global Forces, Local Circumstances and Sustainable Solutions*, Farnham (UK): Gower

McManners, P.J. 2012. *Fly and Be Damned: What now for aviation and climate change?* London: Zed Books.

Meadows, D.H., Meadows, D.L. and Randers, J. 1972. *The Limits to Growth*, New York: Universe Books.

Meadows, D.H., Randers, J. and Meadows, D. 2004. *Limits to Growth: The 30-Year Update*. Vermont: Chelsea Green Publishing Company.

Ministry of Foreign Affairs of Denmark 2013. The World's Leading Wind Energy Hub [Available at: http://www.investindk.com; accessed 16 Nov 2013].

Nature 1995. 'Brent Spar, broken spur', Opinion, *Nature*, Vol 375 : 708.

Nokia 2013. 'The Nokia Story', [http://www.nokia.com/global/about-nokia/about-us/the-nokia-story/; accessed 3 Dec 2013].

OFT 2006. 'Payment protection insurance market study: emerging issues', Report dated August 2006 [available at: http://www.oft.gov.uk/shared_oft/investigations/payment.pdf; accessed 19 Aug 2013].

Peck, S.W. 2011. *Investment Ethics*, Hoboken, New Jersey: John Wiley & Sons.

Porter, M.E. 1979. 'How Competitive Forces Shape Strategy', *Harvard Business Review*: March/April 1979: 137–145.

Porter, M.E., 1980. *Competitive strategy: Techniques for analyzing industries and competitors*, New York: The Free Press.

Pressman E.R. (Producer) and Stone, O. (Director) (1987). Wall Street [film], United States: 20th Century Fox.

Railnews 2012. 'Branson to step up attack on DfT today', 10 Sep 2012, [http://www.railnews.co.uk/news/2012/09/10-branson-to-step-up-attack.html; accessed 4 Dec 2013].

Riversimple 2013. 'Our purpose' [http://www.riversimple.com; accessed 11 Nov 2013].

Rubenstein, D. and Kealey, J. (2012) Cooperation, Conflict, and the Evolution of Complex Animal Societies. *Nature Education Knowledge*, 3(10): 78.

Ruddick, G. 2011. 'Is there still life in Southern Cross?' *The Telegraph*, 5 June 2011. [http://www.telegraph.co.uk/finance/newsbysector/epic/sche/8556612/Is-there-still-life-in-Southern-Cross.html; accessed 10 Nov 2013].

Sabbagh, D. 2006. 'Blackstone prepares £1bn flotation of Southern Cross', *The Times*, 2 Jan 2006 [http://www.thetimes.co.uk; accessed 10 Nov 2013].

Schumpeter, J.A. 1994. (first published 1942) *Capitalism, Socialism and Democracy*, London: Routledge.

Serra, N., Spiegel, S. and Stiglitz, J.E. 2008. 'Introduction: From the Washington Consensus: Towards a New Global Governance', in *The Washington Consensus Reconsidered: Towards a New Global Governance,* Serra, N. and Stiglitz, J. E. (eds), Oxford: Oxford University Press.

Shell 2008. Shell energy scenarios to 2050, [http://www.shell.com/global/future-energy/scenarios; accessed 20 Nov 2013].

Shell 2013. New Lens Scenarios: a Shift in perspective for a world in transition, [http://www.shell.com/global/future-energy/scenarios; accessed 20 Nov 2013].

Smith, K.G., Carroll, S.J. and Ashford, S.J. 1995. 'Intra- and Interorganizational Cooperation: Toward a Research Agenda', *Academy of Management Journal*, Feb 1995 38: 1 7–23.

Sorensen, T. 2008. *Counselor: A Life at the Edge of History*, New York: Harper.

Stern, N. 2010. 'China's growth, China's cities, and the new global low-carbon industrial revolution', London: Centre for Climate Change and Economics Policy paper, Nov 2010, Grantham Research Institute on Climate and the Environment [http://www.cccep.ac.uk/Publications/Policy/docs/PPStern_China-industrial -rev_Nov10.pdf; accessed 7 Jan 2014].

Stiglitz, J.E. 2010. *The Stiglitz Report: Reforming the International Monetary and Financial Systems in the Wake of the Global Crisis*, New York: The New Press.

Stout, L. 2012. *The Shareholder Value Myth*, San Francisco: Berrett-Koehler.

Swift, J. 1726. *Travels into Several Remote Nations of the World. In four parts. By Lemuel Gulliver, First Surgeon, and then a Captain of several Ships*. London: Benjamin Motte.

Taleb, N.N. 2007. *The Black Swan: the impact of the highly improbable*, London: Allen Lane.

Taleb, N.N. 2012. 'From fat tails to Fat Tony', in *The World In 2013*, London: *The Economist*.

Tormey, S. (2012). 'Anti-capitalism' in George Ritzer (ed.), *The Wiley-Blackwell Encyclopedia of Globalization*, UK: Wiley-Blackwell Publishing: 69–71.

Tovstiga, G. 2010. *Strategy in Practice: A Practitioner's Guide to Strategic Thinking*, Chichester: John Wiley & Sons.

US Senate and House of Representatives 2002. Sarbanes-Oxley Act of 2002, Public Law 107–204, 107th Congress, Washington: Government Printing Office.

Vance, A. 2013. 'Revealed: Elon Musk Explains the Hyperloop, the Solar-Powered High-Speed Future of Inter-City Transportation' [http://www.businessweek. com/articles/2013-08-12/revealed-elon-musk-explains-the-hyperloop; accessed 20 Nov 2013].

Vise, D.A. 2005. *The Google Story*, New York: Bantam Dell.

VR Group 2013. 'VR Group – a modern service company', [http://www.vrgroup. fi/en/; accessed 4 Dec 2013].

Webster, A. 2013. *The Twilight of the East India Company: The Evolution of Anglo-Asian Commerce and Politics, 1790–1860*. Woodbridge (UK): The Boydell Press.

Wellings, R. 2013. 'Why are rail subsidies so high?' Institute of Economic Affairs Blog, 12 Jan 2013 [Available at: http://www.iea.org.uk/blog/why-are-rail-subsidies-so-high; accessed 12 Nov 2013].

Williams, J. 2008. 'A Short History of the Washington Consensus', in *The Washington Consensus Reconsidered: Towards a New Global Governance*, Serra, N. and Stiglitz, J.E. (eds), Oxford: Oxford University Press.

Yergin, D. 1991. *The Prize: The Epic Quest for Oil, Money, and Power*, New York: Free Press.

INDEX

For Product Safety Concerns and Information please contact our EU
representative GPSR@taylorandfrancis.com Taylor & Francis Verlag GmbH,
Kaufingerstraße 24, 80331 München, Germany

Printed and bound by CPI Group (UK) Ltd, Croydon, CR0 4YY
01/05/2025
01858395-0001